BREAD MACHINE
RECIPES

*Over 200 Recipes for Making Many Types
of Tasty Bread at Home*

LORY CAMPBELL

LORY CAMPBELL

Table of Contents

Sommario

TABLE OF CONTENTS..5

INTRODUCTION.. 11

BASIC BREAD 14

    PERFECT SANDWICH BREAD 15
    MUSTARD SOUR CREAM BREAD 17
    ITALIAN RESTAURANT STYLE BREADSTICKS.............. 18
    GLUTEN-FREE WHITE BREAD 21
    PERFECT COCOA BREAD.. 23
    SLIDER BUNS 25
    SOUTHERN CORNBREAD 27
    LOW-CARB MULTIGRAIN BREAD 29
    BLACK FOREST LOAF 30
    VEGAN WHITE BREAD 32
    MULTIGRAIN OLIVE OIL WHITE BREAD 33
    EXTRA BUTTERY WHITE BREAD 35
    HONEY WHOLE-WHEAT SANDWICH BREAD............ 37
    GLUTEN-FREE SIMPLE SANDWICH BREAD 39
    BAGELS 40
    100 PERCENT WHOLE-WHEAT BREAD 43
    CLASSIC WHITE BREAD I.. 44
    MEDITERRANEAN SEMOLINA BREAD 46
    OATMEAL WALNUT BREAD.. 48
    MUSTARD FLAVOURED GENERAL BREAD................. 50
    BUTTERMILK WHITE BREAD... 52
    COUNTRY WHITE BREAD.. 54
    BUTTERMILK HONEY BREAD....................................... 56
    CRUSTY FRENCH BREAD 58
    CHOCOLATE CHIP BANANA BREAD 60
    RICE FLOUR RICE BREAD 62
    COCONUT FLOUR BREAD 64
    CRACKED WHEAT BREAD.. 66
    ITALIAN WHITE BREAD.. 68
    ORANGE DATE BREAD 70
    PUMPKIN RAISIN BREAD... 72
    WHOLE WHEAT BREAKFAST BREAD.......................... 73

CHEESE & SWEET BREAD 75

    CHOCO CHIP PUMPKIN BREAD.................................... 76

ITALIAN CHEESE BREAD 78
CHEESY CHIPOTLE BREAD 80
CHOCOLATE ORANGE BREAD 81
CITRUS BREAD 83
MEXICAN STYLE JALAPENO CHEESE BREAD 85
MILK SWEET BREAD 88
DELICIOUS PUMPKIN BREAD 90
BASIL CHEESE BREAD 92
PEACH BREAD 94
OLIVE CHEESE BREAD 95
OLIVE AND CHEDDAR LOAF 97
GINGER SPICED BREAD 99
BLUE CHEESE BREAD 102
COTTAGE CHEESE BREAD 104
CHEDDAR CHEESE BASIL BREAD 106
TRIPLE CHOCOLATE BREAD 108
SWEET VANILLA BREAD 110
MOZZARELLA-HERB BREAD 112
OLIVE LOAF BREAD 114
CHOCOLATE CHIP PEANUT BUTTER BANANA BREAD 116
CRUSTY MUSTARD FOCACCIA 118
OREGANO CHEESE BREAD 120
COCOUT GINGER BREAD 122
GLUTEN-FREE CHEESY BREAD 124
PARMESAN CHEDDAR BREAD 126
COTTAGE CHEESE AND CHIVE BREAD 128
AMERICAN CHEESE BEER BREAD 130
FRENCH CHEESE BREAD 132
PARMESAN CHEESE BREAD 134
DRY FRUIT BREAD 136
CHEESE JALAPENO BREAD 137

FRUIT AND VEGETABLE BREAD **139**

CHOCOLATE-CHERRY BREAD 140
APPLE SPICE BREAD 142
CORNMEAL BREAD 144
ZUCCHINI SPICE BREAD 145
DELICIOUS APPLE BREAD 148
GLUTEN-FREE CINNAMON RAISIN BREAD 150
BANANA WHOLE-WHEAT BREAD 152
POTATO BREAD 154
CRANBERRY WALNUT WHEAT BREAD 155
HONEY POTATO FLAKES BREAD 157
HOT RED PEPPER BREAD 160
GARLIC OLIVE BREAD 161
GLUTEN-FREE BEST-EVER BANANA BREAD 164
ONION CHIVE BREAD 166

SQUASH CARROT BREAD 168
BANANA SPLIT LOAF 171
LIGHT CORN BREAD 173
POTATO HONEY BREAD 175
ZUCCHINI BREAD 177
BLACK OLIVE BREAD 179
RAISIN CANDIED FRUIT BREAD 181
BLUEBERRY HONEY BREAD 183
CARROT CORIANDER BREAD 185
BROWN BREAD WITH RAISINS 187
BLUEBERRIES 'N ORANGE BREAD 189
FRENCH ONION BREAD 191
FRESH BLUEBERRY BREAD 193
GINGER-CARROT-NUT BREAD 195
APPLE-FIG BREAD WITH HONEY GLAZE 197
CHAI-SPICED BREAD 200
HARVEST FRUIT BREAD 202
BLUEBERRY-BASIL LOAF 204

CLASSIC DAILY BREAD **205**
OAT QUINOA BREAD 206
LEMON CAKE 209
CLASSIC WHOLE WHEAT BREAD 211
GARLIC CHEESE PULL-APART ROLLS 214
DONUTS 216
EVERYTHING BAGEL LOAF 218
PEANUT BUTTER BREAD 220
PIZZA DOUGH 222
10 MINUTE ROSEMARY BREAD 224
MULTIGRAIN LOAF 226
FLAXSEED MILK BREAD 228
GARLIC PEPPERONI BREAD 230
BUTTERMILK BREAD 231
COFFEE RYE BREAD 233
APPLE WALNUT BREAD 235
HONEY WHEAT BREAD 237
CHOCOLATE CHIP BREAD 240
SAUSAGE HERB AND ONION BREAD 242
CARROT CAKE BREAD 243
TEXAS ROADHOUSE ROLLS 245
PIZZA ROLLS 247
PANETTONE 249
HONEY WHOLE WHEAT BREAD 251
CHOCOLATE MARBLE CAKE 253
CHOCOLATE COFFEE BREAD 255
CLASSIC WHITE BREAD 257
INSANE COFFEE CAKE 259

MULTIGRAIN HONEY BREAD 261
GOLDEN TURMERIC CARDAMOM BREAD 263
CINNAMON PECAN COFFEE CAKE 265
OAT BRAN MOLASSES BREAD.. 267

SPICE, NUT & HERB BREAD 268

SEED BREAD.. 269
HAZELNUT HONEY BREAD.. 271
FLAXSEED HONEY BREAD 272
HEALTHY SPELT BREAD 274
QUINOA WHOLE-WHEAT BREAD.. 276
TACO BREAD... 278
GARLIC, HERB, AND CHEESE BREAD 280
DILLY ONION BREAD 281
MOLASSES CANDIED-GINGER BREAD... 283
SUNFLOWER & FLAX SEED BREAD 285
HONEY-SPICE EGG BREAD 287
MIX SEED RAISIN BREAD 288
HERB AND PARMESAN BREAD 290
CHIA SEED BREAD 292
ORANGE ALMOND BACON BREAD.. 294
CHOCOLATE MINT BREAD 295
ITALIAN PINE NUT BREAD.. 297
ANISE LEMON BREAD 299
EGG AND SEED BUNS 301
OLIVE BREAD 303
CINNAMON BREAD 305
OATMEAL SEED BREAD 307
WHOLE-WHEAT SEED BREAD 309
GARLIC HERB BREAD... 311
PESTO NUT BREAD 313
SESAME FRENCH BREAD.. 315
COFFEE RAISIN BREAD 317
SEMOLINA BREAD 319
GINGERED SPICE BREAD.. 321
NUTTY WHEAT BREAD 323
SAVOURY HERB BLEND BREAD 325
PUMPKIN COCONUT ALMOND BREAD.. 326

AD FROM AROUND THE WORLD 328

"PO BOY" ROLLS FROM NEW ORLEANS 329
HEALTHY LOW CARB BREAD... 330
RUSSIAN RYE BREAD 332
SAUERKRAUT BREAD.. 334
CORN POPPY SEEDS SOUR CREAM BREAD... 336
FRENCH HAM BREAD 338
MEXICAN SWEETBREAD 339

MEDITERRANEAN BREAD 341
MATCHA COCONUT COOKIES 343
PITA BREAD 345
SWEET DINNER ROLLS 347
PIZZA DOUGH RECIPE 349
GARLIC AND HERB BREAD 350
SWEET CHALLA 352
CHALLAH 354
ZESTY POPPY SEED BREAD 356
NO-BAKE BUTTER COOKIES 358
RAISIN BREAD 360
COUNTRY-STYLED WHITE BREAD 362
ITALIAN HERB PIZZA DOUGH 364
RICE BREAD 366
WALNUT BREAD 368
KETO PUMPKIN BREAD 370
WHITE CHOCOLATE BREAD 372
EUROPEAN BLACK BREAD 374
CINNAMON BUTTER COOKIES 376
PORTUGESE SWEET BREAD 378
BRITISH HOT CROSS BUNS 380
AMISH WHEAT BREAD 383
SWEDISH CARDAMOM BREAD 385
VANILLA MILK BREAD 387
GERMAN PUMPERNICKEL BREAD 389

OTHER BREAD MACHINE RECIPES 390

COCOA BANANA BREAD 391
SWEDISH COFFEE BREAD 393
QUINOA OATMEAL BREAD 394
CHEESEBUTTERMILK BREAD 396
PEANUT BUTTER BREAD 397
JALAPENO CHEDDAR BREAD 399
SLIDER BUNS 402
ONION BREAD 405
HAMBURGER BUNS 407
RAISIN BREAD 410
LOAF OF GLUTEN-FREE SANDWICHES 412
BANANA AND LEMON BREAD 414
CHEESE AND HERB BREAD 416
SUN VEGETABLE BREAD 419
MILK AND HONEY BREAD 420
SPICED HERB BREAD 422
WHOLE WHEAT BREAD GLUTEN FREE 424
CORN BREAD 426
LOW-SODIUM BREAD 428
NO-YEAST SOURDOUGH STARTER 430

GLUTEN FREE BREAD FOR SANDWICHES 432
CHOCOLATE ZUCCHINI BREAD 434
BREAD WITH SPINACH AND FETA 436
BREAD WITH PUMPKIN AND RAISINS 438
NO-SALT WHITE BREAD 440
ROSEMARY BREAD 442
SWEET PINEAPPLE BREAD 444
SEMOLINA BREAD 446
VANILLA BREAD 448
POTATO HONEY BREAD 450
SAUSAGE HERB AND ONION BREAD 452
ANISE LEMON BREAD 453
RICE FLOUR BREAD 455
PARMESAN CHEESE BREAD 457
BLUEBERRY BREAD 459
CHOCOLATE COFFEE BREAD 461
ITALIAN WHITE BREAD 463

Introduction

Here's why your kitchen needs a bread machine

With a handy bread machine, you can make homemade bread and other dough-based dishes in just a few hours.

If you love the taste, smell, and texture of freshly baked bread - especially when it's homemade - you need a bread machine in your collection of kitchen tools.

Everything a bread machine can do

Many bread machines on the market can make a 2-pound loaf of crusty, chewy, soft bread. The best part is that it does all the work for you.

A bread machine can do more than just bake your standard loaf of bread. The possibilities are endless once you get used to working with it. It can be used to make countless appetizers, side dishes, and meals, from gooey cinnamon rolls to soft dinner rolls, from Indian-style naan to Belgian-style soft pretzels, and every doughy recipe in between.

Most bread machines have a kneading function, which can be used to knead the dough, pizza, and more. You can even bake a warm, moist cake in a bread machine.

Bread machines bake at a fairly low temperature, which makes them great for making many dishes that can typically be done in a slow cooker. It has several functions that can be used for a variety of recipes. You can also make jams, as well as sauces, stews, soups, even scrambled eggs and yogurt.

To help inspire your creations, we've collected a few dozen tasty recipes you can use a bread machine with.

BASIC BREAD

Perfect Sandwich Bread

Servings: 10

Cooking Time: 2 Hours

Ingredients:
All-purpose flour – 4 cups
Olive oil – 2 tbsps.
Yeast – 2 tsps.
Honey – 1 ½ tsp.
Warm water – 1 ¾ cups
Salt – 1 tsp

Directions:
Add water, honey, salt, olive oil, flour, and yeast into the bread
machine pan. Select basic/white bread setting then select light/medium
crust and start. Once loaf is done, remove the loaf pan from the
machine. Allow it to cool for 5 minutes. Slice and serve.

Nutrition Info: Calories 335, Total Fat 9g, Saturated Fat 1.7g,
Cholesterol 24g, Sodium 514mg

LORY CAMPBELL

Mustard Sour Cream Bread

Servings: 1 Loaf

Cooking Time: 1 Hour

Ingredients:
1¼ cups (320 ml) lukewarm milk
Three tablespoons sunflower oil
Three tablespoons sour cream
Two tablespoons dry mustard
One egg
½ sachet sugar vanilla
4 cups (690 g) wheat flour
One teaspoon active dry yeast
Two tablespoons white sugar
Two teaspoons sea salt

Directions:
Prepare all of the ingredients for your bread and measuring means (a cup, a spoon, kitchen scales).
Carefully measure the ingredients into the pan.
Put all the ingredients into a bread bucket in the right order, follow your manual for the bread machine.
Cover it. Select the program of your bread machine to BASIC and choose the crust colour to MEDIUM.
Press START. Wait until the program completes.
When done, take the bucket out and let it cool for 5-10 minutes.
Shake the loaf from the pan and let cool for 30 minutes on a cooling rack.
Slice, serve and enjoy the taste of fragrant homemade bread.

Nutrition Info: Calories 340, Total Fat 9.2g, Saturated Fat 1.9g, Cholesterol 26g, Sodium 614mg

Italian Restaurant Style Breadsticks

Servings: 12 - 16

Cooking Time: 3 Hours

Ingredients:
1/2 cups warm water
tablespoons butter, unsalted and melted
4 1/4 cups bread flour
2 tablespoons sugar
1 tablespoon salt
1 package active dry yeast
For the topping:
stick unsalted butter, melted
teaspoons garlic powder
1 teaspoons salt
1 teaspoon par

Directions:

Add wet ingredients to your bread maker pan.

Mix dry ingredients, except yeast, and add to pan.

Make a well in the center of the dry ingredients and add the yeast.

Set to Dough cycle and press Start.

When the dough is done, roll out and cut into strips; keep in mind that they will double in size after they have risen, so roll them out thinner than a typical breadstick to yield room for them to grow.

Place on a greased baking sheet.

Cover the dough with a light towel and let sit in a warm area for 45 minutes to an hour.

Preheat an oven to 400°F.

Bake breadsticks for 6 to 7 minutes.

Mix the melted butter, garlic powder, salt and parsley in a small mixing bowl.

Brush the bread sticks with half the butter mixture; return to oven and bake for 5 to 8 additional minutes.

Remove breadsticks from the oven and brush the other half of the butter mixture.

Allow to cool for a few minutes before serving.

Nutrition Info: Calories: 148, Sodium: 450mg, Dietary Fiber: 1g, Fat: 2.5g, Carbs: 27.3g, Protein: 3.7g

Gluten-free White Bread

Servings: 14 Slices

Cooking Time: 3 H.

Ingredients:
2 eggs
1⅓ cups milk
6 Tbsp oil
1 tsp vinegar
3⅝ cups white bread flour
tsp salt
Tbsp sugar
2 tsp dove farm quick yeast

Directions:
Add each ingredient to the bread machine in the order and at the temperature recommended by your bread machine manufacturer.
Close the lid and start the machine on the gluten free bread program, if available. Alternatively use the basic or rapid setting with a dark crust option.
When the bread machine has finished baking, remove the bread and put it on a cooling rack.

Nutrition Info: Calories: 120, Sodium: 113 mg, Dietary Fiber: 0.8g, Fat: 2.1 g, Carbs: 21.7 g, Protein: 3.4 g

Perfect Cocoa Bread

Servings: 10

Cooking Time: 3 Hours

Ingredients:
Milk – 1 cup.
Egg – 1
Egg yolk – 1
Olive oil – 3 tbsps.
Vanilla extract – 1 tsp.
Salt – 1 tsp.
Bread flour – 3 cups.
Brown sugar – ½ cup.
Cocoa powder – 1/3 cup.
Vital wheat gluten – 1 tbsp.
Yeast – 2 ½ tsps.

Directions:
Add all ingredients into the bread machine pan. Select basic setting then select medium crust and start. Once loaf is done, remove the loaf pan from the machine. Allow it to cool for 10 minutes. Slice and serve.

Nutrition Info: Calories: 118, Sodium: 111 mg, Dietary Fiber: 0.8g, Fat: 2.0 g, Carbs: 20.7 g, Protein: 3.1 g

Slider Buns

Servings: 18

Cooking Time: 3 Hours

Ingredients:
1 1/4 cups milk
egg
tablespoons butter
3/4 teaspoon salt
1/4 cup white sugar
3/4 cups all-purpose flour
1 package active dry yeast
Flour, for surface

Directions:
Add all ingredients to the pan of your bread maker in the order listed above.
Set bread machine to Dough cycle. Once the Dough cycle is complete, roll dough out on a floured surface to about a 1-inch thickness.
Cut out 18 buns with a biscuit cutter or small glass and place them on a greased baking sheet.
Let buns rise about one hour or until they have doubled in size.
Bake at 350°F for 10 minutes.
Brush the tops of baked buns with melted butter and serve.

Nutrition Info: Calories: 130, Sodium: 118mg, Dietary Fiber: 0.8g, Fat: 2.2g, Carbs: 23.7g, Protein: 3.7g

Southern Cornbread

Servings: 10

Cooking Time: 1 Hour

Ingredients:
2 fresh eggs, at room temperature
1 cup milk
1/4 cup butter, unsalted, at room temperature
3/4 cup sugar
teaspoon salt
cups unbleached all-purpose flour
1 cup cornmeal
1 tablespoon baking powder

Directions:
Add all of the ingredients to your bread maker in the order listed.
Select the Quick Bread cycle, light crust color, and press Start.
Allow to cool for five minutes on a wire rack and serve warm.

Nutrition Info: Calories: 258, Sodium: 295mg, Dietary Fiber: 1.6g,
Fat: 6.7g, Carbs: 45.4g, Protein: 5.5g

Low-carb Multigrain Bread

Servings: 1 Loaf

Cooking Time: 1 Hour And 30 Minutes

Ingredients:
¾ cup whole-wheat flour
¼ cup cornmeal
¼ cup oatmeal
Two tablespoons 7-grain cereals
Two tablespoons baking powder
One teaspoon salt
¼ teaspoon baking soda
¾ cup of water
¼ cup of vegetable oil
¼ cup of orange juice
Three tablespoons aquafaba

Directions:
In the bread pan, add the wet ingredients first, then the dry ingredients.
Press the "Quick" or "Cake" mode of your bread machine.
Wait until all cycles are through.
Remove the bread pan from the machine.
Let the bread rest for 10 minutes in the pan before taking it out to cool down further.
Slice the bread after an hour has passed.

Nutrition Info: Calories: 60, Carbohydrates: 9g, Fat: 2g, Protein: 1g

Black Forest Loaf

Servings: 1 Loaf

Cooking Time: 3 Hours

Ingredients:
1 ½ cups bread flour
1 cup whole wheat flour
1 cup rye flour
Three tablespoons cocoa
One tablespoon caraway seeds
Two teaspoons yeast
1 ½ teaspoons salt
One ¼ cups water
1/3 cup molasses
1 ½ tablespoon canola oil

Directions:
Combine the ingredients in the bread pan by putting the wet ingredients first, followed by the dry ones.
Press the "Normal" or "Basic" mode and light the bread machine's crust colour setting.
After the cycles are completed, take out the bread from the machine. Cooldown and then slice the bread.

Nutrition Info: Calories: 136, Carbohydrates: 27g, Fat: 2g, Protein: 3g

Vegan White Bread

Servings: 14 Slices

Cooking Time: 3 H.

Ingredients:
1⅓ cups water
⅓ cup plant milk (I use silk soy original)
1½ tsp salt
2 Tbsp granulated sugar
2 Tbsp vegetable oil
3½ cups all-purpose flour
1¾ tsp bread machine yeast

Directions:
Add each ingredient to the bread machine in the order and at the temperature recommended by your bread machine manufacturer.
Close the lid, select the basic or white bread, medium crust setting on your bread machine, and press start.
When the bread machine has finished baking, remove the bread and put it on a cooling rack.

Nutrition Info: Calories: 126, Carbohydrates: 32g, Fat: 4g, Protein: 3g

Multigrain Olive Oil White Bread

Servings: 1 Loaf (16 Slices)

Cooking Time: 1 Hour And 30 Minutes

Ingredients:
For the Dough
300 ml water
500 grams bakers flour
8 grams dried yeast
10 ml salt
5 ml caster suger
40 ml olive oil
For the Seed mix
40 grams sunflower seeds
20 grams sesame seeds
20 grams flax seeds
20 grams quinoa
20 grams pumpkin seeds

Directions:
For the water: to 100ml of boiling water add 200ml of cold water.
Add the ingredients in the order required by the manufacturer.
add the seeds at the time required by your machine.
Empty dough onto a floured surface and gently use your finger tips to push some of the air out of it. Shape however you like and place on or in an oiled baking tray. Sprinkle with flour or brush with egg for a glazed finish. Slash the top. Cover and rise for 30 mins. Heat oven to 240C/220C fan/gas. Bake for 30-35 mins until browned and crisp.

Nutrition Info: Calories 114.1, Total Fat 3.1g, Saturated Fat 0.5g Polyunsaturated Fat 0.4g, Monounsaturated Fat 1.9g, Sodium 83.4mg, Potassium 0.0 mg, Total Carbohydrate 19.7 g

Extra Buttery White Bread

Servings: 16 Slices

Cooking Time: 3 H. 10 Min.

Ingredients:
1⅛ cups milk
4 Tbsp unsalted butter
3 cups bread flour
1½ Tbsp white granulated sugar
1½ tsp salt
1½ tsp bread machine yeast

Directions:
Soften the butter in your microwave.
Add each ingredient to the bread machine in the order and at the temperature
recommended by your bread machine manufacturer.
Close the lid, select the basic or white bread, medium crust setting on your bread machine, and press start.
When the bread machine has finished baking, remove the bread and put it on a cooling rack.

Nutrition Info: Calories: 146, Carbohydrates: 42g, Fat: 6g, Protein: 5g

Honey Whole-wheat Sandwich Bread

Servings: 14 Slices

Cooking Time: 3 H.

Ingredients:
4¼ cups whole-wheat flour
½ tsp salt
1½ cups water
¼ cup honey
2 Tbsp olive oil, or melted butter
2¼ tsp bread machine yeast (1 packet)

Directions:
Add each ingredient to the bread machine in the order and at the temperature recommended by your bread machine manufacturer.
Close the lid, select the whole wheat, low crust setting on your bread machine and press start.
When the bread machine has finished baking, remove the bread and put it on a cooling rack.

Nutrition Info: Calories: 116, Carbohydrates: 22g, Fat: 4.6g, Protein: 3.5g

Gluten-free Simple Sandwich Bread

Servings: 1 Loaf

Cooking Time: 10 Minutes

Ingredients:
1 1/2 cups sorghum flour
cup tapioca starch or potato starch (not potato flour)
1/2 cup gluten-free millet flour or gluten-free oat flour
teaspoons xanthan gum
1/4 teaspoons fine sea salt
1/2 teaspoons gluten-free yeast for bread machines
1 1/4 cups warm water
3 tablespoons extra virgin olive oil
tablespoon honey or raw agave nectar
1/2 teaspoon mild rice vinegar or lemon juice
organic free-range eggs, beaten

Directions:
Preparing the Ingredients
Whisk together the dry ingredients except the yeast and set aside.
Add the liquid ingredients to the bread maker pan first, then gently
pour the mixed dry ingredients on top of the liquid.
Make a well in the center of the dry ingredients and add the yeast.
Select the Bake cycle
Set for Rapid 1 hour 20 minutes, medium crust color, and press Start.
Transfer to a cooling rack for 15 minutes before slicing to serve.

Nutrition Info: Calories: 201, Carbohydrates: 19g, Fat: 8g, Protein: 5g

Bagels

Servings: 9

Cooking Time: 1 Hour

Ingredients:
1 cup warm water
1/2 teaspoons salt
tablespoons sugar
cups bread flour
1/4 teaspoons active dry yeast
quarts boiling water
3 tablespoons white sugar
1 tablespoon cornmeal
1 egg white
Flour, for surface

Directions:

Place in the bread machine pan in the following order: warm water, salt, sugar, and flour.

Make a well in the center of the dry ingredients and add the yeast. Select Dough cycle and press Start.

When Dough cycle is complete, remove pan and let dough rest on a lightly floured surface. Stir 3 tablespoons of sugar into the boiling water.

Cut dough into 9 equal pieces and roll each piece into a small ball. Flatten each ball with the palm of your hand. Poke a hole in the middle of each using your thumb. Twirl the dough on your finger to make the hole bigger, while evening out the dough around the hole.

Sprinkle an ungreased baking sheet with 1 teaspoon cornmeal. Place the bagel on the baking sheet and repeat until all bagels are formed. Cover the shaped bagels with a clean kitchen towel and let rise for 10 minutes.

Preheat an oven to 375°F.

Carefully transfer the bagels, one by one, to the boiling water. Boil for 1 minute, turning halfway.

Drain on a clean towel. Arrange boiled bagels on the baking sheet. Glaze the tops with egg white and sprinkle any toppings you desire. Bake for 20 to 25 minutes or until golden brown.

Let cool on a wire rack before serving.

Nutrition Info: Calories: 185, Sodium: 394mg, Dietary Fiber: 1.4g, Fat: 0.5g, Carbs: 39.7g, Protein: 5.2g

100 Percent Whole-wheat Bread

Servings: 1 Loaf

Cooking Time: 10 Minutes Or Less

Ingredients:
12 slice bread (1½ pound)
1⅛ cups water, at 80°F to 90°F
2¼ tablespoons melted butter, cooled
2¼ tablespoons honey
1⅛ teaspoons salt
3 cups whole-wheat bread flour
2 teaspoons sugar
2 tablespoons skim milk powder
¾ teaspoon salt
1½ teaspoons bread machine or instant yeast

Directions:
Preparing the Ingredients.
Choose the size of bread to prepare. Measure and add the ingredients to the pan in the order as indicated in the ingredient listing. Place the pan in the bread machine and close the lid.
Select the Bake cycle
Turn on the bread maker. Select the Wheat/ Whole setting, then select the dough size and crust color. Press start to start the cycle. When this is done, and the bread is baked, remove the pan from the machine. Let stand a few minutes.
Remove the bread from the pan and leave it on a wire rack to cool for at least 10 minutes. Slice and serve.

Nutrition Info: Calories: 136, Carbohydrates: 27g, Fat: 6g, Protein: 5g

Classic White Bread I

Servings: 1 Loaf

Cooking Time: 10 Minutes

Ingredients:
16 slice bread (2 pounds)
1½ cups lukewarm water
1 tablespoon + 1 teaspoon olive oil
1½ teaspoons sugar
1 teaspoon table salt
¼ teaspoon baking soda
2½ cups all-purpose flour
1 cup white bread flour
2½ teaspoons bread machine yeast

Directions:
Preparing the Ingredients
Choose the size of bread to prepare. Measure and add the ingredients to the pan in the order as indicated in the ingredient listing. Place the pan in the bread machine and close the lid.
Select the Bake cycle
Close the lid, Turn on the bread maker. Select the White / Basic setting, then select the dough size and crust color. Press start to start the cycle.
When this is done, and the bread is baked, remove the pan from the machine. Let stand a few minutes.
Remove the bread from the pan and leave it on a wire rack to cool for at least 10 minutes.
After this time, proceed to cut it

Nutrition Info: Calories: 136, Carbohydrates: 27g, Fat: 2g, Protein: 3g

Mediterranean Semolina Bread

Servings: 1 Loaf (16 Slices)

Cooking Time: 30 Minutes

Ingredients:
1 cup lukewarm water (80 degrees F)
One teaspoon salt
2½ tablespoons butter, melted
2½ teaspoons white sugar
2¼ cups all-purpose flour
1/3 cups semolina
1½ teaspoons active dry yeast

Directions:
Prepare all of the ingredients for your bread and measuring means (a cup, a spoon, kitchen scales).
Carefully measure the ingredients into the pan.
Put all the ingredients into a bread bucket in the right order. Follow your manual for the bread machine.
Close the cover.
Select your bread machine's program to ITALIAN BREAD / SANDWICH mode and choose the crust colour to MEDIUM.
Press START. Wait until the program completes.
When done, take the bucket out and let it cool for 5-10 minutes.
Shake the loaf from the pan and let cool for 30 minutes on a cooling rack.
Slice and serve.

Nutrition Info: Calories 243, Total Fat 8.1g, Saturated Fat 4.9g, Cholesterol 20g, Sodium 203mg, Total Carbohydrate 37g, Dietary Fiber 1.5g, Total Sugars 2.8g, Protein 5.3g

Oatmeal Walnut Bread

Servings: 1 Loaf

Cooking Time: 1 Hour And 30 Minutes

Ingredients:
¾ cup whole-wheat flour
¼ cup all-purpose flour
½ cup brown sugar
1/3 cup walnuts, chopped
¼ cup oatmeal
¼ teaspoon of baking soda
Two tablespoons baking powder
One teaspoon salt
1 cup Vegan buttermilk
¼ cup of vegetable oil
Three tablespoons aquafaba

Directions:
Add into the bread pan the wet ingredients then followed by the dry ingredients.
Use the "Quick" or "Cake" setting of your bread machine.
Allow the cycles to be completed.
Take out the pan from the machine.
Wait for 10 minutes, then remove the bread from the pan.
Once the bread has cooled down, slice it and serve.

Nutrition Info: Calories: 80, Carbohydrates: 11g, Fat: 3g, Protein: 2g

Mustard Flavoured General Bread

Servings: 2 Loaves

Cooking Time: 40 Minutes

Ingredients:
1¼ cups milk
Three tablespoons sunflower milk
Three tablespoons sour cream
Two tablespoons dry mustard
One whole egg beaten
½ sachet sugar vanilla
4 cups flour
One teaspoon dry yeast
Two tablespoons sugar
Two teaspoon salt

Directions:
Take out the bread maker's bucket and pour in milk and sunflower oil stir and then add sour cream and beaten egg.
Add flour, salt, sugar, mustard powder, vanilla sugar, and mix well.
Make a small groove in the flour and sprinkle the yeast.
Transfer the bucket to your bread maker and cover.
Set the program of your bread machine to Basic/White Bread and set crust type to Medium.
Press START.
Wait until the cycle completes.
Once the loaf is ready, take the bucket out and let it cool for 5 minutes.
Gently shake the bucket to remove the loaf. 10. Transfer to a cooling rack, slice, and serve.

Nutrition Info: Calories: 340 Cal, Fat: 10g, Carbohydrates: 54g, Protein: 10g, Fibre: 1g

Buttermilk White Bread

Servings: 1 Loaf

Cooking Time: 25 Minutes

Ingredients:
1 1/8 cups water
Three teaspoon honey
One tablespoon margarine
1 1/2 teaspoon salt
3 cups bread flour
Two teaspoons active dry yeast
Four teaspoons powdered buttermilk

Directions:
Into the bread machine's pan, place the ingredients in the order suggested by the manufacturer: select medium crust and white bread settings. You can use a few yeasts during the hot and humid months of summer.

Nutrition Info: Calories: 34 calories, Total Carbohydrate: 5.7g, Cholesterol: 1mg, Total Fat: 1g, Protein: 1g, Sodium: 313mg

Country White Bread

Servings: 2 Loaves

Cooking Time: 45 Minutes

Ingredients:
Two teaspoons active dry yeast
1 1/2 tablespoon sugar
4 cups bread flour
1 1/2 teaspoon salt
One large egg
1 1/2 tablespoon butter
1 cup warm milk, with a temperature of 110 to 115 degrees F (43 to 46 degrees C)

Directions:
Put all the liquid ingredients in the pan. Add all the dry ingredients except the yeast. Use your hand to form a hole in the middle of the dry ingredients. Put the yeast in the spot. 2.   Secure the pan in the chamber and close the lid. Choose the basic setting and your preferred crust colour—press start.
Once done, transfer the baked bread to a wire rack. Slice once cooled.

Nutrition Info: Calories: 105 calories, Total Carbohydrate: 0g, Total Fat: 0g, Protein: 0g

Buttermilk Honey Bread

Servings: 14 Slices

Cooking Time: 3 H. 35 Min.

Ingredients:
½ cup water
¾ cup buttermilk
¼ cup honey
3 Tbsp butter, softened and cut into pieces
3 cups bread flour
1½ tsp salt
2¼ tsp yeast (or 1 package)

Directions:
Add each ingredient to the bread machine in the order and at the temperature recommended by your bread machine manufacturer. Close the lid, select the basic bread, medium crust setting on your bread machine and press start.
When the bread machine has finished baking, remove the bread and put it on a cooling rack.

Nutrition Info: Calories: 116, Carbohydrates: 23g, Fat: 3g, Protein: 4g

Crusty French Bread

Servings: 1 Loaf

Cooking Time: 10 Minutes

Ingredients:
12 slice bread (1½ pound)
cup water, at 80°F to 90°F
1¼ tablespoons olive oil
tablespoons sugar
1¼ teaspoons salt
cups white bread flour
1¼ teaspoons bread machine or instant yeast, or flax seeds (optional)

Directions:
Preparing the Ingredients.
Place the ingredients in your bread machine as recommended by the manufacturer.
Select the Bake cycle
Program the machine for French bread, select light or medium crust, and press Start.
When this is done, and the bread is baked, remove the pan from the machine. Let stand a few minutes.
Remove the bread from the pan and leave it on a wire rack to cool for at least 10 minutes.

Nutrition Info: Calories: 125, Carbohydrates: 24g, Fat: 3g, Protein: 3.5g

Chocolate Chip Banana Bread

Servings: 1 Loaf

Cooking Time: 10 Minutes

Ingredients:
Shortening or gluten-free cooking spray, for preparing the pan
250 grams All-Purpose Flour Blend
1 teaspoon ground cinnamon
1 teaspoon xanthan gum
teaspoon baking powder
½ teaspoon baking soda
¼ teaspoon salt
large eggs
1 teaspoon vanilla extract
90 grams mini semisweet chocolate chips or nondairy alternative
80 grams plain Greek yogurt or nondairy alternative
450 grams mashed bananas (about 4 large bananas)
8 tablespoons (1 stick) butter or nondairy alternative
150 grams light brown sugar

Directions:
Preparing the Ingredients.
Measure and add the ingredients to the pan in the order mentioned above. Place the pan in the bread machine and close the lid.
Select the Bake cycle
Close the lid, Turn on the bread maker. Select the White / Basic setting, then select the dough size, select light or medium crust. Press start to start the cycle.
When this is done, and the bread is baked, remove the pan from the machine. Let the bread cool in the pan for at least 20 minutes, then gently transfer it to a wire rack to cool completely.

Nutrition Info: Calories: 154, Carbohydrates: 6g, Protein: 8g, Fat: 16g

Rice Flour Rice Bread

Servings: 16 Slices

Cooking Time: 3 H. 15 Min.

Ingredients:
3 eggs
1½ cups water
3 Tbsp vegetable oil
1 tsp apple cider vinegar
2¼ tsp active dry yeast
3¼ cups white rice flour
2½ tsp xanthan gum
1½ tsp salt
½ cup dry milk powder
3 Tbsp white sugar

Directions:
In a medium-size bowl, mix the eggs, water, oil, and vinegar.
In a large bowl, add the yeast, salt, xanthan gum, dry milk powder, rice flour, and sugar. Mix with a whisk until incorporated.
Add each ingredient to the bread machine in the order and at the temperature recommended by your bread machine manufacturer.
Close the lid, select the whole wheat, medium crust setting on your bread machine, and press start.
When the bread machine has finished baking, remove the bread and put it on a cooling rack.

Nutrition Info: Calories: 143, Carbohydrates: 4.5g, Protein: 7.3g, Fat: 13g

Coconut Flour Bread

Servings: 12 Pcs

Cooking Time: 15 Minutes

Ingredients:
6 eggs
1/2 cup coconut flour
2 tbsp psyllium husk
1/4 cup olive oil
1 1/2 tsp salt
1 tbsp xanthan gum
tbsp baking powder
1/4 tsp yeast

Directions:
Use a small bowl to combine all of the dry ingredients except for the yeast.
In the bread machine pan, add all the wet ingredients.
Add all of your dry ingredients from the small mixing bowl to the bread machine pan.
Top with the yeast.
Set the machine to the basic setting.
When the bread is finished, remove the bread machine pan from the bread machine.
Let cool slightly before transferring to a cooling rack.
It can be stored for four days on the counter and up to 3 months in the freezer.

Nutrition Info: Calories: 174, Carbohydrates: 4g, Protein: 7g, Fat: 15g

Cracked Wheat Bread

Servings: 10

Cooking Time: 1 Hour 20 Minutes

Ingredients:
1/4 cup plus 1 tablespoon water
2 tablespoons vegetable oil
2 cups bread flour
3/4 cup cracked wheat
1/2 teaspoons salt
tablespoons sugar
2 1/4 teaspoons active dry yeast

Directions:
Bring water to a boil.
Place cracked wheat in small mixing bowl, pour water over it and stir.
Cool to 80°F.
Place cracked wheat mixture into pan, followed by all ingredients (except yeast) in the order listed.
Make a well in the center of the dry ingredients and add the yeast.
Select the Basic Bread cycle, medium color crust, and press Start.
Check dough consistency after 5 minutes of kneading. The dough should be a soft, tacky ball. If it is dry and stiff, add water one 1/2 tablespoon at a time until sticky. If it's too wet and sticky, add 1 tablespoon of flour at a time.
Remove bread when cycle is finished and allow to cool before serving.

Nutrition Info: Calories: 232, Sodium: 350mg, Dietary Fiber: 3.3g, Fat: 3.3g, Carbs: 43.7g, Protein: 6.3g

Italian White Bread

Servings: 14 Slices

Cooking Time: 3 H.

Ingredients:
¾ cup cold water
2 cups bread flour
1 Tbsp sugar
1 tsp salt
1 Tbsp olive oil
1 tsp active dry yeast

Directions:
Add each ingredient to the bread machine in the order and at the temperature recommended by your bread machine manufacturer.
Close the lid, select the Italian or basic bread, low crust setting on your bread machine, and press start.
When the bread machine has finished baking, remove the bread and put it on a cooling rack.

Nutrition Info: Calories: 148, Carbohydrates: 5g, Protein: 9g, Fat: 13g

Orange Date Bread

Servings: 1 Loaf

Cooking Time: 1 Hour And 30 Minutes

Ingredients:
2 cups all-purpose flour
1 cup dates, chopped
¾ cup of sugar
½ cup walnuts, chopped
Two tablespoons orange rind, grated
1 ½ teaspoons baking powder
One teaspoon baking soda
½ cup of orange juice
½ cup of water
One tablespoon vegetable oil   One teaspoon vanilla extract

Directions:
Put the wet ingredients then the dry ingredients into the bread pan.
Press the "Quick" or "Cake" mode of the bread machine.
Allow all cycles to be finished.
Remove the pan from the machine, but keep the bread in the pan for
10 minutes more.
Take out the bread from the pan, and let it cool down completely
before slicing.

Nutrition Info: Calories: 80, Carbohydrates: 14g, Fat: 2g, Protein: 1g

Pumpkin Raisin Bread

Servings: 1 Loaf

Cooking Time: 1 Hour And 30 Minutes

Ingredients:
½ cup all-purpose flour
½ cup whole-wheat flour
½ cup pumpkin, mashed
½ cup raisins
¼ cup brown sugar
Two tablespoons baking powder
One teaspoon salt
One teaspoon pumpkin pie spice
¼ teaspoon baking soda
¾ cup apple juice
¼ cup of vegetable oil
Three tablespoons aquafaba

Directions:
Place all ingredients in the bread pan in this order: apple juice, pumpkin, oil, aquafaba, flour, sugar, baking powder, baking soda, salt, pumpkin pie spice, and raisins.
Select the "Quick" or "Cake" mode of your bread machine.
Let the machine finish all cycles.
Remove the pan from the machine.
After 10 minutes, transfer the bread to a wire rack.
Slice the bread only when it has completely cooled down.

Nutrition Info: Calories: 70, Carbohydrates: 12g, Fat: 2g, Protein: 1g

Whole Wheat Breakfast Bread

Servings: 14 Slices

Cooking Time: 3 H. 5 Min.

Ingredients:
3 cups white whole wheat flour
½ tsp salt
1 cup water
½ cup coconut oil, liquified
4 Tbsp honey
2½ tsp active dry yeast

Directions:
Add each ingredient to the bread machine in the order and at the temperature recommended by your bread machine manufacturer.
Close the lid, select the basic bread, medium crust setting on your bread machine and press start.
When the bread machine has finished baking, remove the bread and put it on a cooling rack.

Nutrition Info: Calories: 135, Carbohydrates: 3g, Protein: 4g, Fat: 11g

CHEESE & SWEET BREAD

Choco Chip Pumpkin Bread

Servings: 10

Cooking Time: 2 Hours

Ingredients:
Eggs – 2
Chocolate chips – 1/3 cup.
Brown sugar – 1 ½ cups.
Vegetable oil – ½ cup.
Can pumpkin puree – 15 oz.
Baking powder – 1 tsp.
Baking soda – 1 tsp.
Cinnamon – 1 tsp.
Pumpkin pie spice – 2 tsps.
All-purpose flour – 2 cups.
Salt – ½ tsp.

Directions:
Add all ingredients except for chocolate chips into the bread machine pan. Select quick bread setting then select light crust and press start. Add chocolate chips just before the final kneading cycle. Once loaf is done, remove the loaf pan from the machine. Allow it to cool for 10 minutes. Slice and serve.

Nutrition Info: Calories: 58, Carbohydrates: 6g, Fat: 2g, Protein: 1g

Italian Cheese Bread

Servings: 14 Slices

Cooking Time: 10 Minutes

Ingredients:
1¼ cups water
3 cups bread flour
½ shredded pepper jack cheese
2 tsp Italian seasoning
2 Tbsp brown sugar
1½ tsp salt
2 tsp active dry yeast

Directions:
Preparing the Ingredients.
Add each ingredient to the bread machine in the order and at the temperature recommended by your bread machine manufacturer.
Select the Bake cycle
Close the lid, select the basic bread, medium crust setting on your bread machine, and press start.
When the bread machine has finished baking, remove the bread and put it on a cooling rack.

Nutrition Info: Calories: 56, Carbohydrates: 7.3g, Fat: 2.5g, Protein:1g

Cheesy Chipotle Bread

Servings: 1 Loaf

Cooking Time: 10 Minutes

Ingredients:
8 slice bread (1 pounds)
⅔ cup water, at 80°F to 90°F
1½ tablespoons sugar
1½ tablespoons powdered skim milk
¾ teaspoon salt
½ teaspoon chipotle chili powder
2 cups white bread flour
½ cup (2 ounces) shredded sharp Cheddar cheese
¾ teaspoon bread machine or instant yeast

Directions:
Preparing the Ingredients.
Choose the size of loaf of your preference and then measure the ingredients.
Add all of the ingredients mentioned previously in the list.
Close the lid after placing the pan in the bread machine.
Select the Bake cycle
Turn on the bread machine. Select the White/Basic setting, select the loaf size, and the crust color. Press start.
When the cycle is finished, carefully remove the pan from the bread maker and let it rest.
Remove the bread from the pan, put in a wire rack to Cool about 5 minutes. Slice

Nutrition Info: Calories: 62, Carbohydrates: 9.3g, Fat: 2.3g, Protein: 1.6g

Chocolate Orange Bread

Servings: 14 Slices

Cooking Time: 10 Minutes Plus Fermenting Time

Ingredients:
1⅝ cups strong white bread flour
2 Tbsp cocoa
1 tsp ground mixed spice
egg, beaten
½ cup water
¼ cup orange juice
Tbsp butter
Tbsp light muscovado sugar
1 tsp salt
1½ tsp easy bake yeast
¾ cup mixed peel
¾ cup chocolate chips

Directions:
Preparing the Ingredients
Sift the flour, cocoa, and spices together in a bowl.
Add each ingredient to the bread machine in the order and at the temperature recommended by your bread machine manufacturer.
Select the Bake cycle
Close the lid, select the sweet loaf, medium crust setting on your bread machine, and press start.
Add the mixed peel and chocolate chips 5 to 10 minutes before the last kneading cycle ends.
When the bread machine has finished baking, remove the bread and put it on a cooling rack.

Nutrition Info: Calories: 72, Carbohydrates: 8.3g, Fat: 3.3g, Protein: 1.8g

Citrus Bread

Servings: 10

Cooking Time: 3 Hours And 25 Minutes

Ingredients:
1 whole egg
Butter - 3 tbsp., melted
White sugar - 1/3 cup
Vanilla sugar - 1 tbsp.
Tangerine juice - ½ cup
Whole milk - 2/3 cup
Kosher salt - 1 tsp.
Bread machine flour - 4 cups
Bread machine yeast - 1 tbsp.
Candied oranges - ¼ cup
Candied lemon - ¼ cup
Lemon zest -2 tsp., finely grated
Almonds - ¼ cup, chopped

Directions:
Add everything in the bread machine (except fruits, zest, and almonds) according to bread machine recommendations.
Select Basic/Sweetbread and Medium crust.
Add zest, fruits, and chopped almonds after the beep.
Remove the bread when done.
Cool, slice, and serve.

Nutrition Info: Calories: 404, Total Fat: 9.1 g,
Saturated Fat: 3.5 g, Carbohydrates: 71.5 g, Cholesterol: 34 mg,
Fiber: 2.9 g, Calcium: 72 mg, Sodium: 345 mg, Protein: 9.8 g

LORY CAMPBELL

Mexican Style Jalapeno Cheese Bread

Servings: 1 Loaf

Ingredients:
16 slice bread (2 pounds)
1 small jalapeno pepper, seeded and minced
1 cup lukewarm water
3 tablespoons nonfat dry milk powder
1½ tablespoons unsalted butter, melted
1½ tablespoons sugar
1½ teaspoons table salt
¼ cup finely shredded cheese (Mexican blend or Monterrey Jack)
3 cups white bread flour
2 teaspoons bread machine yeast
12 slice bread (1½ pounds)
small jalapeno pepper, seeded and minced
¾ cup lukewarm water
tablespoons nonfat dry milk powder
1 tablespoon unsalted butter, melted
1 tablespoon sugar
1 teaspoon salt
3 tablespoons finely shredded cheese (Mexican blend or Monterrey Jack)
2 cups white bread flour
1½ teaspoons bread machine yeast

Directions:
Choose the size of loaf you would like to make and measure your ingredients.
Add the ingredients to the bread pan in the order listed above.
Place the pan in the bread machine and close the lid.
Turn on the bread maker. Select the White/Basic setting, then the loaf size, and finally the crust color. Start the cycle.
When the cycle is finished and the bread is baked, carefully remove the pan from the machine. Use a potholder as the handle will be very hot. Let rest for a few minutes.
Remove the bread from the pan and allow to cool on a wire rack for at least 10 minutes before slicing.

Nutrition Info: (Per Serving): Calories 220, fat 9.4g, carbs 18.6g, sodium 206mg, protein 9g

Milk Sweet Bread

Servings: 1 Loaf

Ingredients:
16 slice bread (2 pounds)
1⅓ cups lukewarm milk
1 egg, at room temperature
2⅔ tablespoons butter, softened
⅔ cup sugar
1⅓ teaspoons table salt
4 cups white bread flour
2¼ teaspoons bread machine yeast
12 slice bread (1½ pounds)
1 cup lukewarm milk
egg, at room temperature
tablespoons butter, softened
½ cup sugar
1 teaspoon table salt
3 cups white bread flour
2¼ teaspoons bread machine yeast

Directions:
Choose the size of loaf you would like to make and measure your ingredients.
Add the ingredients to the bread pan in the order listed above.
Place the pan in the bread machine and close the lid.
Turn on the bread maker. Select the Sweet setting, then the loaf size, and finally the crust color. Start the cycle.
When the cycle is finished and the bread is baked, carefully remove the pan from the machine. Use a potholder as the handle will be very hot. Let rest for a few minutes.
Remove the bread from the pan and allow to cool on a wire rack for at least 10 minutes before slicing.

Nutrition Info: (Per Serving): Calories 178, fat 3.2g, carbs 32.6g, sodium 227mg, protein 4.8g

—
88

Delicious Pumpkin Bread

Servings: 10

Cooking Time: 2 Hours

Ingredients:
All-purpose flour – 3 cups.
Ground ginger – ¼ tsp.
Ground nutmeg – ¼ tsp.
Ground cinnamon – ¾ tsp.
Baking soda – ½ tsp.
Baking powder – 1 ½ tsps.
Granulated sugar – 1 cup.
Pumpkin puree – 1 ½ cups.
Eggs – 3
Olive oil – 1/3 cup
Salt – ¼ tsp.

Directions:
Add all ingredients into the bread machine pan. Select basic setting then select light crust and press start. Once loaf is done, remove the loaf pan from the machine. Allow it to cool for 10 minutes. Slice and serve.

Nutrition Info: (Per Serving): Calories 168, fat 3.3g, carbs 31.6g, sodium 237mg, protein 3.8g

Basil Cheese Bread

Servings: 1 Loaf

Cooking Time: 10 Minutes Plus Fermenting Time

Ingredients:
12 slice bread (1½ pounds)
1 cup lukewarm milk
1 tablespoon unsalted butter, melted
1 tablespoon sugar
1 teaspoon dried basil
¾ teaspoon table salt
¾ cup sharp Cheddar cheese, shredded
3 cups white bread flour
1½ teaspoons bread machine yeast

Directions:
Preparing the Ingredients.
Choose the size of loaf of your preference and then measure the ingredients.
Add all of the ingredients mentioned previously in the list.
Close the lid after placing the pan in the bread machine.
Select the Bake cycle
Turn on the bread machine. Select the Quick/Rapid setting, select the loaf size, and the crust color. Press start.
When the cycle is finished, carefully remove the pan from the bread maker and let it rest. 8.   Remove the bread from the pan, put in a wire rack to Cool about 5 minutes. Slice

Nutrition Info: Calories: 226, Carbohydrates: 22g, Fat: 3g, Protein: 4g

Peach Bread

Servings: 10

Cooking Time: 3 Hours And 48 Minutes

Ingredients:
Wholemeal flour – 4 cups
Bread machine yeast – 2 tsp.
Lukewarm water – 1 ¼ cups
Flaxseed oil – 1 ½ tsp.
Brown sugar – 1 ½ tsp.
Kosher salt – 1 ½ tsp.
Peaches – 2, peeled and diced

Directions:
Add everything in the bread machine (except the peaches) according to bread machine recommendations.
Select Whole-Grain and Medium crust.
Add the peaches after the beep.
Remove the bread when done.
Cool, slice, and serve.

Nutrition Info: (Per Serving): Calories: 246, Total Fat: 4g, Saturated Fat: 0.3g, Carbohydrates: 44.3g, Cholesterol: 0mg, Fiber: 6.4g, Calcium: 50mg, Sodium: 440mg, Protein: 8.2 g

Olive Cheese Bread

Servings: 8 Pcs

Cooking Time: 15 Minutes

Ingredients:
2/3 cup milk, set at 80°F to 90°F
One tablespoon melted butter cooled
2/3 Teaspoon minced garlic
One tablespoon sugar
2/3 teaspoon salt
2 cups white bread flour
½ cup (2 ounces) shredded Swiss cheese
¾ teaspoon bread machine or instant yeast
¼ cup chopped black olives

Directions:
Place the ingredients in your device as recommended on it.
Make a program on the machine for basic white Bread, select Light or medium crust, and press Start.
When the loaf is finished, remove the bucket from the machine.
Let the loaf cool for a minute.
Gently shake the bucket and remove the loaf and turn it out onto a rack to cool.

Nutrition Info: Calories: 175 calories, Total Carbohydrate: 27g, Total Fat: 5g, Protein: 6g, Sodium: 260 mg

Olive And Cheddar Loaf

Servings: 1 Loaf

Cooking Time: 45 Minutes

Ingredients:
1 cup water, room temperature
Four teaspoons sugar
¾ teaspoon salt
1 and 1/ cups sharp cheddar cheese, shredded
3 cups bread flour
Two teaspoons active dry yeast
¾ cup pimiento olives, drained and sliced

Directions:
Add the listed ingredients to your bread machine (except salami), following the
manufactures instructions.
Set the bread machine's program to Basic/White Bread and the crust type to light. Press Start.
Let the bread machine work and wait until it beeps this your indication to add the remaining ingredients. At this point, add the salami.
Wait until the remaining bake cycle completes.
Once the loaf is done, take the bucket out from the bread machine and let it rest for 5 minutes.
Gently shake the bucket and remove the loaf, transfer the loaf to a cooling rack and slice.
Serve and enjoy!

Nutrition Info: Calories: 124 calories, Total Carbohydrate: 19g, Total Fat: 4g, Protein: 5g, Sugar: 5g

Ginger Spiced Bread

Servings: 1 Loaf

Ingredients:
16 slice bread (2 pounds)
1⅓ cups lukewarm buttermilk
1 egg, at room temperature
⅓ cup dark molasses
4 teaspoons unsalted butter, melted
¼ cup sugar
2 teaspoons table salt
4¼ cups white bread flour
2 teaspoons ground ginger
1¼ teaspoons ground cinnamon
⅔ teaspoon ground nutmeg
⅓ teaspoon ground cloves
2¼ teaspoons bread machine yeast
12 slice bread (1½ pounds)
1 cup lukewarm buttermilk
1 egg, at room temperature
¼ cup dark molasses
1 tablespoon unsalted butter, melted
3 tablespoons sugar
1½ teaspoons table salt
3½ cups white bread flour
teaspoon ground cinnamon
½ teaspoon ground nutmeg
¼ teaspoon ground cloves
1½ teaspoons ground ginger
teaspoons bread machine yeast

Directions:
Choose the size of loaf you would like to make and measure your ingredients.
Add the ingredients to the bread pan in the order listed above.
Place the pan in the bread machine and close the lid.
Turn on the bread maker. Select the Sweet setting, then the loaf size, and finally the crust color. Start the cycle.
When the cycle is finished and the bread is baked, carefully remove the pan from the machine. Use a potholder as the handle will be very hot. Let rest for a few minutes.
Remove the bread from the pan and allow to cool on a wire rack for at least 10 minutes before slicing.

Nutrition Info: (Per Serving): Calories 187, fat 2.3g, carbs 36.7g, sodium 312mg, protein 4.6g

Blue Cheese Bread

Servings: 12 Slices

Cooking Time: 10 Minutes

Ingredients:
3/4 cup warm water
1 large egg
1 teaspoon salt
3 cups bread flour
cup blue cheese, crumbled
tablespoons nonfat dry milk
2 tablespoons sugar
1 teaspoon bread machine yeast

Directions:
Preparing the Ingredients
Add the ingredients to bread machine pan in the order listed above, (except yeast) ; be sure to add the cheese with the flour.
Make a well in the flour; pour the yeast into the hole.
Select the Bake cycle
Select Basic bread cycle, medium crust color, and press Start.
When finished, transfer to a cooling rack for 10 minutes and serve warm.

Nutrition Info: Calories: 203, Carbohydrates: 28g, Fat: 3g, Protein: 4g

Cottage Cheese Bread

Servings: 1 Loaf

Cooking Time: 45 Minutes

Ingredients:
1/2 cup water
1 cup cottage cheese
Two tablespoons margarine
One egg
One tablespoon white sugar
1/4 teaspoon baking soda
One teaspoon salt
3 cups bread flour
2 1/2 teaspoons active dry yeast

Directions:
Into the bread machine, place the ingredients according to the
ingredients list's order, then push the start button. In case the dough
looks too sticky, feel free to use up to half a cup more bread flour.

Nutrition Info: Calories: 171, Total Carbohydrate: 26.8g,
Cholesterol: 18mg,Total Fat: 3.6g, Protein: 7.3g, Sodium: 324 mg

Cheddar Cheese Basil Bread

Servings: 1 Loaf

Cooking Time: 10 Minutes

Ingredients:
12 slice bread (1½ pounds)
1 cup milk, at 80°F to 90°F
1 tablespoon melted butter, cooled
1 tablespoon sugar
1 teaspoon dried basil
¾ cup (3 ounces) shredded sharp Cheddar cheese
¾ teaspoon salt
3 cups white bread flour
1½ teaspoons bread machine or active dry yeast

Directions:
Preparing the Ingredients.
Choose the size of loaf of your preference and then measure the ingredients.
Add all of the ingredients mentioned previously in the list.
Close the lid after placing the pan in the bread machine.
Select the Bake cycle
Turn on the bread machine. Select the White/Basic setting, select the loaf size, and the crust color. Press start.
When the cycle is finished, carefully remove the pan from the bread maker and let it rest.
Remove the bread from the pan, put in a wire rack to Cool about 5 minutes. Slice

Nutrition Info: Calories: 216, Carbohydrates: 25g, Fat: 5g, Protein: 6g

Triple Chocolate Bread

Servings: 1 Loaf

Cooking Time: 10 Minutes Plus Fermenting Time

Ingredients:
8 slices bread (1 pound)
⅔ cup milk, at 80°F to 90°F
1 egg, at room temperature
1½ tablespoons melted butter, cooled
teaspoon pure vanilla extract
tablespoons light brown sugar
tablespoon unsweetened cocoa powder
½ teaspoon salt
cups white bread flour
1 teaspoon bread machine or instant yeast
¼ cup semisweet chocolate chips
¼ cup white chocolate chips

Directions:
Preparing the Ingredients.
Place the ingredients, except the chocolate chips, in your bread machine as recommended by the manufacturer.
Select the Bake cycle
Program the machine for Basic/White bread, select light or medium crust, and press Start.
When the machine signals, add the chocolate chips, or put them in the nut/raisin hopper and the machine will add them automatically.
When the loaf is done, remove the bucket from the machine.
Let the loaf cool for 5 minutes.
Gently shake the bucket to remove the loaf, and turn it out onto a rack to cool.

Nutrition Info: Calories: 146, Carbohydrates: 20g, Fat: 4.5g, Protein: 4g

Sweet Vanilla Bread

Servings: 1 Loaf

Cooking Time: 10 Minutes Plus Fermenting Time

Ingredients:
12 slice bread (1½ pounds)
½ cup + 1 tablespoon lukewarm milk
3 tablespoons unsalted butter, melted
3 tablespoons sugar
1 egg, at room temperature
1½ teaspoons pure vanilla extract
⅓ teaspoon almond extract
2½ cups white bread flour
1½ teaspoons bread machine yeast

Directions:
Preparing the Ingredients.
Choose the size of loaf you would like to make and measure your ingredients.
Add the ingredients to the bread pan in the order listed above.
Place the pan in the bread machine and close the lid.
Select the Bake cycle
Turn on the bread maker. Select the White/Basic setting, then the loaf size, and finally the crust color. Start the cycle.
When the cycle is finished and the bread is baked, carefully remove the pan from the machine. Use a potholder as the handle will be very hot. Let rest for a few minutes.
Remove the bread from the pan and allow to cool on a wire rack for at least 10 minutes before slicing.

Nutrition Info: Calories: 116, Carbohydrates: 17g, Fat: 3g, Protein: 4g

Mozzarella-herb Bread

Servings: 1 Loaf

Cooking Time: 10 Minutes Plus Fermenting Time

Ingredients:
12 slice bread (1½ pounds)
1¼ cups milk, at 80°F to 90°F
tablespoon butter, melted and cooled
tablespoons sugar
teaspoon salt
teaspoons dried basil
1 teaspoon dried oregano
1½ cups (6 ounces) shredded mozzarella cheese
3 cups white bread flour
2¼ teaspoons bread machine or instant yeast

Directions:
Preparing the Ingredients.
Choose the size of loaf of your preference and then measure the ingredients.
Add all of the ingredients mentioned previously in the list.
Close the lid after placing the pan in the bread machine.
Select the Bake cycle
Turn on the bread machine. Select the Quick/Rapid setting, select the loaf size, and the crust color. Press start.
When the cycle is finished, carefully remove the pan from the bread maker and let it rest.
Remove the bread from the pan, put in a wire rack to Cool about 5 minutes. Slice

Nutrition Info: Calories: 123, Carbohydrates: 30g, Fat: 4g, Protein: 5g

Olive Loaf Bread

Servings: 1 Loaf

Cooking Time: 10 Minutes Plus Fermenting Time

Ingredients:
1 cup plus 2 tablespoons water
1 tablespoon olive oil
3 cups bread flour
2 tablespoons instant nonfat dry milk
1 tablespoon sugar
1/4 teaspoons salt
1/4 teaspoon garlic powder
teaspoons active dry yeast
2/3 cup grated parmesan cheese
1 cup pitted Greek olives, sliced and drained

Directions:
Preparing the Ingredients
Add ingredients, except yeast, olives and cheese, to bread maker in order listed above. Make a well in the flour; pour the yeast into the hole.
Select the Bake cycle
Select Basic cycle, light crust color, and press Start; do not use delay cycle.Just before the final kneading, add the olives and cheese. Remove and allow to cool on a wire rack for 15 minutes before serving.

Nutrition Info: Calories: 172, Carbohydrates: 31g, Fat: 4g, Protein: 5.5g

Chocolate Chip Peanut Butter Banana Bread

Servings: 1 Loaf

Cooking Time: 10 Minutes Plus Fermenting Time

Ingredients:
12 to 16 slice bread (1½ to 2 pounds)
2 bananas, mashed
2 eggs, at room temperature
½ cup melted butter, cooled
2 tablespoons milk, at room temperature
teaspoon pure vanilla extract
cups all-purpose flour
½ cup sugar
1¼ teaspoons baking powder
½ teaspoon baking soda
½ teaspoon salt
½ cup peanut butter chips
½ cup semisweet chocolate chips

Directions:
Preparing the Ingredients.
Stir together the bananas, eggs, butter, milk, and vanilla in the bread machine bucket and set it aside. In a medium bowl, toss together the flour, sugar, baking powder, baking soda, salt, peanut butter chips, and chocolate chips. Add the dry ingredients to the bucket.
Select the Bake cycle. Program the machine for Quick/Rapid bread, and press Start.
When the loaf is done, stick a knife into it, and if it comes out clean, the loaf is done.
If the loaf needs a few more minutes, check the control panel for a Bake Only button and extend the time by 10 minutes.
When the loaf is done, remove the bucket from the machine. Let the loaf cool for 5 minutes.
Gently shake the bucket to remove the loaf, and turn it out onto a rack to cool.

Nutrition Info: Calories: 146, Carbohydrates: 32g, Fat: 4g, Protein: 5g

Crusty Mustard Focaccia

Servings: 8 Slices

Cooking Time: 10 Minutes Plus Fermenting Time

Ingredients:
2/3 cup water
tablespoon olive or vegetable oil
tablespoons spicy mustard
2¼ cups bread flour
1 tablespoon sugar
1 teaspoon table salt
1½ teaspoons bread machine or fast-acting dry yeast
3 tablespoons olive or vegetable oil
Coarse (kosher or sea) salt, if desired

Directions:
Preparing the Ingredients.
Measure carefully, placing all ingredients except 3 tablespoons oil and the coarse salt in bread machine pan in the order recommended by the manufacturer.
Select Dough/Manual cycle. Do not use delay cycle.
Remove dough from pan, using lightly floured hands. Knead 5 minutes on lightly floured surface (if necessary, knead in enough additional flour to make dough easy to handle). Cover and let rest 10 minutes.
Select the Bake cycle
Grease large cookie sheet. Roll or pat dough into 12-inch round on cookie sheet. Cover and let rise in warm place 10 minutes or until almost double.
Heat oven to 400°F. Prick dough with fork at 1-inch intervals or make deep depressions in dough with fingertips. Brush with 3 tablespoons oil. Sprinkle with coarse salt. Bake 15 to 18 minutes or until golden brown. Serve warm or cool.

Nutrition Info: Calories: 201, Carbohydrates: 34, Fat: 5g, Protein: 7g

Oregano Cheese Bread

Servings: 1 Loaf

Cooking Time: 10 Minutes

Ingredients:
3 cups bread flour
1 cup water
½ cup freshly grated parmesan cheese
3 Tbsp sugar
1 Tbsp dried leaf oregano
1½ Tbsp olive oil
tsp salt
tsp active dry yeast

Directions:
Preparing the Ingredients
Add each ingredient to the bread machine in the order and at the temperature recommended by your bread machine manufacturer.
Select the Bake cycle
Close the lid, select the basic bread, medium crust setting on your bread machine, and press start.
When the bread machine has finished baking, remove the bread and put it on a cooling rack.

Nutrition Info: Calories: 185, Carbohydrates: 33g, Fat: 6.5g, Protein: 7g

Cocout Ginger Bread

Servings: 1 Loaf

Cooking Time: 1 Hour

Ingredients:
1 cup + 2 tbsp Half & Half
One ¼ cup toasted shredded coconut
Two large eggs
¼ cup oil
1 tsp coconut extract
1 tsp lemon extract
3/4 cup sugar
tbsp grated lemon peel
cups all-purpose flour
2 tbsp finely chopped candied ginger
1 tbsp baking powder
½ tsp salt
One ¼ cup toasted shredded coconut

Directions:
Put everything in your bread machine pan.
Select the quick bread mode.
Press the start button.
Allow bread to cool on the wire rack until ready to serve (at least 20 minutes).

Nutrition Info: Calories 210, Carbohydrates: 45g, Total Fat 3g, Cholesterol 3mg, Protein 5g, Fiber 2g, Sugar 15g, Sodium 185mg, Potassium 61mg

Gluten-free Cheesy Bread

Servings: 10

Cooking Time: 4 Hours

Ingredients:
Eggs – 3
Olive oil – 2 tbsps.
Water – 1 ½ cups.
Active dry yeast – 2 ¼ tsp.
White rice flour – 2 cups.
Brown rice flour – 1 cup.
Milk powder – ¼ cup.
Sugar – 2 tbsps.
Poppy seeds – 1 tbsp.
Xanthan gum – 3 ½ tsps.
Cheddar cheese – 1 ½ cups., shredded
Salt – 1 tsp.

Directions:
In a medium bowl, mix together eggs, water, and oil and pour it into the bread machine pan. In a large bowl, mix together remaining ingredients and pour over wet ingredient mixture into the bread pan. Select whole wheat setting then select light/medium crust and start. Once loaf is done, remove the loaf pan from the machine. Allow it to cool for 10 minutes. Slice and serve.

Nutrition Info: Calories: 184, Carbohydrates: 9g, Protein: 8g, Fat: 12g

Parmesan Cheddar Bread

Servings: 1 Loaf

Cooking Time: 10 Minutes Plus Fermenting Time

Ingredients:
12 slice bread (1½ pounds)
1¼ cups lukewarm milk
tablespoon unsalted butter, melted
tablespoons sugar
1 teaspoon table salt
½ teaspoon freshly ground black pepper
Pinch cayenne pepper
1½ cups shredded aged sharp Cheddar cheese
½ cup shredded or grated Parmesan cheese
3 cups white bread flour
1¼ teaspoons bread machine yeast

Directions:
Preparing the Ingredients.
Choose the size of loaf of your preference and then measure the ingredients.
Add all of the ingredients mentioned previously in the list.
Close the lid after placing the pan in the bread machine.
Select the Bake cycle
Turn on the bread machine. Select the Quick/Rapid setting, select the loaf size, and the crust color. Press start.
When the cycle is finished, carefully remove the pan from the bread maker and let it rest.
Remove the bread from the pan, put in a wire rack to Cool about 5 minutes. Slice

Nutrition Info: Calories: 193, Carbohydrates: 5g, Protein: 9g, Fat: 17g

Cottage Cheese And Chive Bread

Servings: 14 Servings

Cooking Time: 10 Minutes

Ingredients:
³/₈ cup water
1 cup cottage cheese
large egg
Tbsp butter
1½ tsp salt
3¾ cups white bread flour
Tbsp dried chives
2½ Tbsp granulated sugar
2¼ tsp active dry yeast

Directions:
Preparing the Ingredients
Add each ingredient to the bread machine in the order and at the temperature recommended by your bread machine manufacturer.
Select the Bake cycle
Close the lid, select the basic bread, medium crust setting on your bread machine, and press start.
When the bread machine has finished baking, remove the bread and put it on a cooling rack.

Nutrition Info: Calories: 182, Carbohydrates: 6g, Protein: 6g, Fat: 14g

American Cheese Beer Bread

Servings: 1 Loaf

Ingredients:
16 slice bread (2 pounds)
1⅔ cups warm beer
1½ tablespoons sugar
2 teaspoons table salt
1½ tablespoons unsalted butter, melted
¾ cup American cheese, shredded
¾ cup Monterrey Jack cheese, shredded
4 cups white bread flour
2 teaspoons bread machine yeast
12 slice bread (1½ pounds)
1¼ cups warm beer
1 tablespoon sugar
1½ teaspoons table salt
1 tablespoon unsalted butter, melted
½ cup American cheese, shredded
½ cup Monterrey Jack cheese, shredded
3 cups white bread flour
1½ teaspoons bread machine yeast

Directions:
Choose the size of loaf you would like to make and measure your ingredients.
Add the ingredients to the bread pan in the order listed above.
Place the pan in the bread machine and close the lid.
Turn on the bread maker. Select the White/Basic setting, then the loaf size, and finally the crust color. Start the cycle.
When the cycle is finished and the bread is baked, carefully remove the pan from the machine. Use a potholder as the handle will be very hot. Let rest for a few minutes.
Remove the bread from the pan and allow to cool on a wire rack for at least 10 minutes before slicing.

Nutrition Info: (Per Serving): Calories 173, fat 5.3 , carbs 26.1g, sodium 118mg, protein 6.2g

French Cheese Bread

Servings: 14 Slices

Cooking Time: 10 Minutes

Ingredients:
1 tsp sugar
2¼ tsp yeast
1¼ cup water
3 cups bread flour
2 Tbsp parmesan cheese
1 tsp garlic powder
1½ tsp salt

Directions:
Preparing the Ingredients
Add each ingredient to the bread machine in the order and at the temperature recommended by your bread machine manufacturer.
Select the Bake cycle
Close the lid, select the basic bread, medium crust setting on your bread machine, and press start.
When the bread machine has finished baking, remove the bread and put it on a cooling rack.

Nutrition Info: Calories: 144, Carbohydrates: 5g, Protein: 6g, Fat: 16g

Parmesan Cheese Bread

Servings: 8

Cooking Time: 3 Hours And 25 Minutes

Ingredients:
Wheat bread flour - 2½ cups
Fresh bread machine yeast - 1½ tsp.
Whole milk - ½ cup, lukewarm
Butter - 1 tbsp., melted
Sugar - 2 tbsp.
Kosher salt - ½ tsp.
Whole eggs – 2
Fresh/dried rosemary -2 tsp., ground
Parmesan - 3 tbsp. (divided - 2 tbsp. for dough and 1 tbsp. for sprinkling)
Garlic - 2 cloves, crushed

Directions:
Place all the dry and liquid ingredients (except for parmesan, yeast, milk, rosemary, and garlic) in the bread pan according to bread machine recommendations.
Dissolve the yeast in the warm milk and add.
Add the garlic, parmesan, and rosemary after the beep.
Choose Basic cycle and Light crust.
Remove the bread when done.
Cool, slice, and serve.

Nutrition Info: (Per Serving): Calories: 212, Total Fat: 4.6g, Saturated Fat: 2.1g, Carbohydrates: 34.8g, Cholesterol: 49mg, Fiber: 1.5g, Calcium: 18mg, Sodium: 214mg, Protein: 7.6g

Dry Fruit Bread

Servings: 12

Cooking Time: 3 Hours And 25 Minutes

Ingredients:
Water – 1 cup, plus 2 tbsp.
Egg – 1
Butter – 3 tbsp., softened
Packed brown sugar – ¼ cup
Salt – 1 ½ tsp.
Ground nutmeg – ¼ tsp.
Dash allspice
Bread flour – 3 ¾ cups, plus 1 tbsp.
Active dry yeast – 2 tsp.
Dried fruit – 1 cup
Chopped pecans – 1/3 cup

Directions:
Add everything (except fruit and pecans) in the bread machine according to the machine recommendations.
Select Basic bread cycle.
Add fruit and pecans at the beep.
Remove the bread when done.
Cool, slice, and serve.

Nutrition Info: (Per Serving): Calories: 214, Total Fat: 6g, Saturated Fat: 2g, Carbohydrates: 36g, Cholesterol: 25mg, Fiber: 2g, Calcium: 38mg, Sodium: 330mg, Protein: 6g

Cheese Jalapeno Bread

Servings: 10

Cooking Time: 2 Hours

Ingredients:
Monterey jack cheese – ¼ cup, shredded
ùActive dry yeast – 2 tsps.
Butter – 1 ½ tbsps.
Sugar – 1 ½ tbsps.
Milk – 3 tbsps.
Flour – 3 cups.
Water – 1 cup.
Jalapeno pepper – 1, minced
Salt – 1 ½ tsps.

Directions:
Add all ingredients to the bread machine pan according to the bread machine manufacturer instructions. Select basic bread setting then select light/medium crust and start. Once loaf is done, remove the loaf pan from the machine. Allow it to cool for 10 minutes. Slice and serve.

Nutrition Info: Calories: 124, Carbohydrates: 6g, Protein: 5g, Fat: 14g

FRUIT AND VEGETABLE BREAD

Chocolate-cherry Bread

Servings: 1 Loaf

Cooking Time: 10 Minutes

Ingredients:
1½ teaspoons baking powder
½ teaspoon baking soda
¼ teaspoon salt
¾ cup sugar
½ cup butter, softened
2 eggs
1 teaspoon almond extract
1 teaspoon vanilla
1 container (8 oz) sour cream
½ cup chopped dried cherries
½ cup bittersweet or dark chocolate chips

Directions:
Preparing the Ingredients.
Choose the size of loaf of your preference and then measure the ingredients.
Add all of the ingredients mentioned previously in the list. Close the lid after placing the pan in the bread machine.
Select the Bake cycle
Turn on the bread machine. Select the White/Basic setting, select the loaf size, and the crust color. Press start.
When the cycle is finished, carefully remove the pan from the bread maker and let it rest.
Remove the bread from the pan, put in a wire rack to cool for at least 2 hours. Wrap tightly and store at room temperature up to 4 days, or refrigerate.

Nutrition Info: (Per Serving): Calories 146, fat 4.6g, carbs 33.6g, sodium 229mg, protein 3.5g

Apple Spice Bread

Servings: 1 Loaf

Cooking Time: 10 Minutes

Ingredients:
16 slice bread (2 pounds)
1⅓ cup milk, at 80°F to 90°F
3⅓ tablespoons melted butter, cooled
2⅔ tablespoons sugar
2 teaspoons salt
1⅓ teaspoons ground cinnamon
Pinch ground cloves
4 cups white bread flour
2¼ teaspoons bread machine or active dry yeast
1⅓ cups finely diced peeled apple

Directions:
Preparing the Ingredients.
Choose the size of loaf of your preference and then measure the ingredients.
Add all of the ingredients mentioned previously in the list, except for the apple. Close the lid after placing the pan in the bread machine.
Select the Bake cycle
Turn on the bread machine. White/Basic or Fruit/Nut (if your machine has this setting) setting, select the loaf size, and the crust color. Press start.
When the machine signals to add ingredients, add the apple. When the cycle is finished, carefully remove the pan from the bread maker and let it rest.
Remove the bread from the pan, put in a wire rack to cool for at least 10 minutes, and slice.

Nutrition Info: (Per Serving): Calories 172, fat 3.9, carbs 40.6, odium 235mg, protein 3.5g

Cornmeal Bread

Servings: 14 Slices

Cooking Time: 2 H. 10 Min.

Ingredients:
2½ tsp active dry yeast
1⅓ cup water
2 Tbsp dark or light brown sugar
large beaten egg
Tbsp softened butter
1½ tsp salt
¾ cup cornmeal
¾ cup whole wheat flour
2¾ cups white bread flour

Directions:
Add each ingredient to the bread machine in the order and at the temperature recommended by your bread machine manufacturer. Close the lid, select the basic bread, medium crust setting on your bread machine, and press start.
When the bread machine has finished baking, remove the bread and put it on a cooling rack.

Nutrition Info: (Per Serving): Calories 198, fat 4.3g, carbs 28.6g, sodium 227mg, protein 3.7g

Zucchini Spice Bread

Servings: 1 Loaf

Ingredients:
16 slice bread (2 pounds)
2 eggs, at room temperature
⅔ cup unsalted butter, melted
⅔ teaspoon table salt
1 cup shredded zucchini
⅔ cup light brown sugar
3 tablespoons sugar
2 cups all-purpose flour
⅔ teaspoon baking powder
⅔ teaspoon baking soda
⅓ teaspoon ground allspice
1⅓ teaspoons ground cinnamon
⅔ cup chopped pecans
12 slice bread (1½ pounds)
2 eggs, at room temperature
½ cup unsalted butter, melted
½ teaspoon table salt
¾ cup shredded zucchini
½ cup light brown sugar
2 tablespoons sugar
1½ cups all-purpose flour
½ teaspoon baking powder
½ teaspoon baking soda
¼ teaspoon ground allspice
1 teaspoon ground cinnamon
½ cup chopped pecans

Directions:
Choose the size of loaf you would like to make and measure your ingredients.
Add the ingredients to the bread pan in the order listed above.
Place the pan in the bread machine and close the lid.
Turn on the bread maker. Select the Quick/Rapid setting, then the loaf size, and finally the crust color. Start the cycle.
When the cycle is finished and the bread is baked, carefully remove the pan from the machine. Use a potholder as the handle will be very hot. Let rest for a few minutes.
Remove the bread from the pan and allow to cool down on a wire rack for at least 10 minutes or more before slicing.

Nutrition Info: (Per Serving): Calories 167, fat 8.3 g, carbs 19.7 g, sodium 223 mg, protein 3.2 g

Delicious Apple Bread

Servings: 10

Cooking Time: 3 Hours 27 Minutes

Ingredients:
Buttermilk – 1 cup.
Apple juice concentrate – ¼ cup.
Butter – 1 ½ tbsps.
Brown sugar – 3 tbsps.
Ground cinnamon – 1 ½ tsp.
Apples – 1 cup., peeled and chopped
Salt – 1 tsp.
Bread flour – 3 ½ cups.
Vital wheat gluten – 4 tsps.
Yeast – 2 tsps.

Directions:
Add all ingredients to the bread machine as listed order. Select sweet bread setting then select light/medium crust and start. Once loaf is done, remove the loaf pan from the machine. Allow it to cool for 15 minutes. Slice and serve.

Nutrition Info: (Per Serving): Calories 139, fat 3.8g, carbs 33.6g, sodium 241mg, protein 3.6g

Gluten-free Cinnamon Raisin Bread

Servings: 12 Slices

Cooking Time: 5 Minutes

Ingredients:
3/4 cup almond milk
2 tablespoons flax meal
6 tablespoons warm water
1/2 teaspoons apple cider vinegar
tablespoons butter
1 1/2 tablespoons honey
2/3 cups brown rice flour
1/4 cup corn starch
tablespoons potato starch
1 1/2 teaspoons xanthan gum
1 tablespoon cinnamon
1/2 teaspoon salt
1 teaspoon active dry yeast
1/2 cup raisins

Directions:
Preparing the Ingredients
Mix together flax and water and let stand for 5 minutes.
Combine dry ingredients in a separate bowl, except for yeast.
Add wet ingredients to the bread machine.
Add the dry mixture on top and make a well in the middle of the dry mixture.
Add the yeast to the well.
Select the Bake cycle
Set to Gluten Free, light crust color, and press Start. After first kneading and rise cycle, add raisins.
Remove to a cooling rack when baked and let cool for 15 minutes before slicing.

Nutrition Info: (Per Serving): Calories 191, fat 3.6g, carbs 32.6g, sodium 227mg, protein 4.2g

Banana Whole-wheat Bread

Servings: 1 Loaf

Cooking Time: 10 Minutes

Ingredients:
12 slice bread (1½ pounds)
½ cup milk, at 80°F to 90°F
1 cup mashed banana
1 egg, at room temperature
1½ tablespoons melted butter, cooled
3 tablespoons honey
1 teaspoon pure vanilla extract
½ teaspoon salt
1 cup whole-wheat flour
1¼ cups white bread flour
1½ teaspoons bread machine or instant yeast

Directions:
Preparing the Ingredients.
Choose the size of loaf of your preference and then measure the ingredients.
Add all of the ingredients mentioned previously in the list. Close the lid after placing the pan in the bread machine
Select the Bake cycle.
Turn on the bread machine. Select the Sweet bread setting, select the loaf size, and the crust color. Press start. When the cycle is finished, carefully remove the pan from the bread maker and let it rest.
Shake the bucket to remove the loaf, and turn it out onto a rack to cool.

Nutrition Info: (Per Serving): Calories 192, fat 4.8g, carbs 42.6g, sodium 226mg, protein 3.7g

Potato Bread

Servings: 14 Slices

Cooking Time: 3 H. 10 Min.

Ingredients:
¾ cup milk
½ cup water
Tbsp canola oil
1½ tsp salt
cups bread flour
½ cup instant potato flakes
Tbsp sugar
¼ tsp white pepper
tsp active dry yeast

Directions:
Add each ingredient to the bread machine in the order and at the temperature recommended by your bread machine manufacturer. Close the lid, select the basic bread, medium crust setting on your bread machine, and press start.
When the bread machine has finished baking, remove the bread and put it on a cooling rack.

Nutrition Info: (Per Serving): Calories 148, fat 3.0g, carbs 39.6g, sodium 242mg, protein 3.5g

Cranberry Walnut Wheat Bread

Servings: 14 Slices

Cooking Time: 10 Minutes

Ingredients:
1 cup warm water
tablespoon molasses
tablespoons butter
teaspoon salt
cups 100% whole wheat flour
cup unbleached flour
tablespoons dry milk
1 cup cranberries
cup walnuts, chopped
teaspoons active dry yeast

Directions:
Preparing the Ingredients
Add the liquid ingredients to the bread maker pan. Add the dry ingredients, except the yeast, walnuts and cranberries.
Make a well in the center of the bread flour and add the yeast. Insert the pan into your bread maker and secure the lid.
Select the Bake cycle
Select Wheat Bread setting, choose your preferred crust color, and press Start. Add cranberries and walnuts after first kneading cycle is finished. Remove the bread from the oven and turn it out of the pan onto a cooling rack and allow it to cool completely before slicing.

Nutrition Info: Calories: 135, Carbohydrates: 39g, Fat: 5.5g, Protein: 6.2g

Honey Potato Flakes Bread

Servings: 1 Loaf

Ingredients:
16 slice bread (2 pounds)
1⅔ cups lukewarm milk
2⅔ tablespoons unsalted butter, melted
4 teaspoons honey
2 teaspoons table salt
4 cups white bread flour
1½ teaspoons dried thyme
⅔ cup instant potato flakes
2½ teaspoons bread machine yeast
12 slice bread (1½ pounds)
1¼ cups lukewarm milk
2 tablespoons unsalted butter, melted
1 tablespoon honey
1½ teaspoons table salt
3 cups white bread flour
teaspoon dried thyme
½ cup instant potato flakes
teaspoons bread machine yeast

Directions:

Choose the size of loaf you would like to make and measure your ingredients.

Add the ingredients to the bread pan in the order listed above.

Place the pan in the bread machine and close the lid.

Turn on the bread maker. Select the White/Basic setting, then the loaf size, and finally the crust color. Start the cycle.

When the cycle is finished and the bread is baked, carefully remove the pan from the machine. Use a potholder as the handle will be very hot. Let rest for a few minutes.

Remove the bread from the pan and allow to cool on a wire rack for at least 10 minutes before slicing.

Nutrition Info: (Per Serving): Calories 157, fat 3.1g, carbs 27.8g, sodium 294mg, protein 4.8g

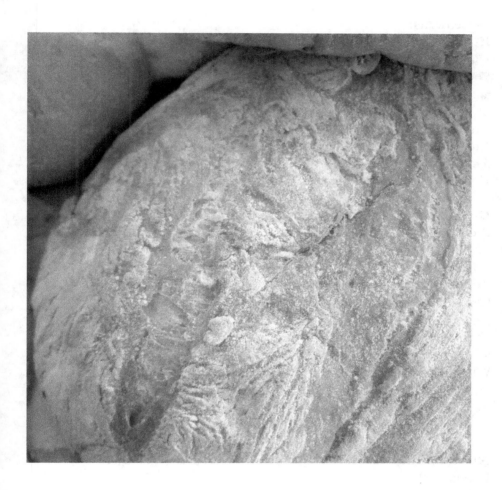

Hot Red Pepper Bread

Servings: 1 Loaf

Cooking Time: 10 Minutes

Ingredients:
12 slice bread (1½ pounds)
1¼ cups milk, at 80°F to 90°F
¼ cup red pepper relish
tablespoons chopped roasted red pepper
tablespoons melted butter, cooled
3 tablespoons light brown sugar
1 teaspoon salt
3 cups white bread flour
1½ teaspoons bread machine or instant yeast

Directions:
Preparing the Ingredients.
Choose the size of loaf of your preference and then measure the ingredients.
Add all of the ingredients mentioned previously in the list.
Close the lid after placing the pan in the bread machine.
Select the Bake cycle
Turn on the bread machine. Select the White/Basic setting, select the loaf size, and the crust color. Press start.
When the cycle is finished, carefully remove the pan from the bread maker and let it rest.
Remove the bread from the pan, put in a wire rack to Cool about 10 minutes. Slice

Nutrition Info: Calories: 133, Carbohydrates: 52g, Fat: 4.8g, Protein: 3.9g

Garlic Olive Bread

Servings: 1 Loaf

Cooking Time: 10 Minutes

Ingredients:
12 slice bread (1½ pounds)
1 cup lukewarm milk
1½ tablespoons unsalted butter, melted
1 teaspoon garlic, minced
1½ tablespoons sugar
1 teaspoon table salt
3 cups white bread flour
1 teaspoon bread machine yeast
⅓ cup black olives, chopped
16 slice bread (2 pounds)
1⅓ cups lukewarm milk
2 tablespoons unsalted butter, melted
1⅓ teaspoons garlic, minced
2 tablespoons sugar
1⅓ teaspoons table salt
4 cups white bread flour
1½ teaspoons bread machine yeast
½ cup black olives, chopped

LORY CAMPBELL

Directions:

Preparing the Ingredients

Choose the size of loaf of your preference and then measure the ingredients.

Add all of the ingredients mentioned previously in the list, except for the olives. Close the lid after placing the pan in the bread machine.

Select the Bake

Turn on the bread machine. White/Basic or Fruit/Nut (if your machine has this setting) setting, select the loaf size, and the crust color. Press start.

When the machine signals to add ingredients, add the olives. When the cycle is finished, carefully remove the pan from the bread maker and let it rest.

Remove the bread from the pan, put in a wire rack to cool for at least 10 minutes, and slice.

Nutrition Info: Calories: 146, Carbohydrates: 38g, Fat: 5g, Protein: 6g

Gluten-free Best-ever Banana Bread

Servings: 1 Loaf

Cooking Time: 10 Minutes

Ingredients:
16 slices bread
½ cup tapioca flour
½ cup white rice flour
½ cup potato starch
¼ cup garbanzo and fava flour
¼ cup sweet white sorghum flour
1 teaspoon xanthan gum
½ teaspoon guar gum
1 teaspoon gluten-free baking powder
1 teaspoon baking soda
1 teaspoon salt
1 teaspoon ground cinnamon
¾ cup packed brown sugar
1 cup mashed very ripe bananas (2 medium)
½ cup ghee (measured melted)
¼ cup almond milk, soymilk or regular milk
teaspoon gluten-free vanilla
eggs

Directions:
Preparing the Ingredients.
Choose the size of loaf of your preference and then measure the
ingredients. Add all of the ingredients mentioned previously in the list.
Close the lid after placing the pan in the bread machine.
Select the Bake cycle Turn on the bread machine. Select the
White/Basic setting, select the loaf size, and the crust color. Press start.
When the cycle is finished, carefully remove the pan from the bread
maker and let it rest. Remove the bread from the pan, put in a wire
rack to Cool about 1 hour.

Nutrition Info: Calories: 116, Carbohydrates: 29g, Fat: 5g, Protein: 3g

Onion Chive Bread

Servings: 1 Loaf

Ingredients:
16 slice bread (2 pounds)
1¼ cups lukewarm water
¼ cup unsalted butter, melted
2 tablespoons sugar
1½ teaspoons table salt
4¼ cups white bread flour
¼ cup dried minced onion
2 tablespoons fresh chives, chopped
2¼ teaspoons bread machine yeast
12 slice bread (1½ pounds)
1 cup lukewarm water
3 tablespoons unsalted butter, melted
1½ tablespoons sugar
1⅛ teaspoons table salt
3⅛ cups white bread flour
3 tablespoons dried minced onion
1½ tablespoons fresh chives, chopped
1⅔ teaspoons bread machine yeast

Directions:
Choose the size of loaf you would like to make and measure your ingredients.
Add the ingredients to the bread pan in the order listed above. Place the pan in the bread machine and close the lid. Turn on the bread maker. Select the White/Basic setting, then the loaf size, and finally the crust color. Start the cycle.
When the cycle is finished and the bread is baked, carefully remove the pan from the machine. Use a potholder as the handle will be very hot. Let rest for a few minutes.
Remove the bread from the pan and allow to cool on a wire rack for at least 10 minutes before slicing.

Nutrition Info: (Per Serving): Calories 147, fat 3g, carbs 26.2g, sodium 223mg, protein 4.6g

Squash Carrot Bread

Servings: 8 Pcs

Cooking Time: 1 Hour And 30 Minutes

Ingredients:
One small zucchini
One baby carrot
1 cup whey
1 ½ cups (180 g) white wheat flour
¾ cup (100 g) whole wheat flour
¾ cup (100 g) rye flour
Two tablespoons vegetable oil
One teaspoon yeast, fresh
One teaspoon salt
½ teaspoon sugar

Directions:

Cut/dice carrots and zucchini to about 8-10 mm (1/2 inch) in size.
In a frying pan, heat the vegetable oil, then fry the vegetables over medium heat until soft. If desired, season the vegetables with salt and pepper.
Transfer the vegetables to a flat plate so that they cool down more quickly. While still hot, they cannot be added to the dough.
Now dissolve the yeast in the serum.
Send all kinds of flour, serum with yeast, as well as salt and sugar to the bakery.
Knead the dough in the dough for the Rolls program.
At the very end of the batch, add the vegetables to the dough.
After adding vegetables, the dough will become moister at the end of the fermentation, which will last about an hour before doubling the dough's volume, shift it onto a thickly floured surface.
Form into a loaf and put it in an oiled form.
Cover the form with a food film and leave for 1 to 1 1/3 hours.
Preheat oven to 450°F and put bread in it.
Bake the bread for 15 minutes, and then gently remove it from the mould. Lay it on the grate and bake for 15-20 minutes more

Nutrition Info: Calories 220, Total Fat 4.3g, Saturated Fat 0.8g, Cholesterol 0g, Sodium 313mg, Total Carbohydrate 39.1g, Dietary Fiber 4.1g, Total Sugars 2.7g, Protein 6.6g

Banana Split Loaf

Servings: 12

Cooking Time: 1 Hour

Ingredients:
2 eggs
1/3 cup butter, melted
2 tablespoons whole milk
2 overripe bananas, mashed
2 cups all-purpose flour
2/3 cups sugar
1 1/4 teaspoons baking powder
1/2 teaspoon baking soda
1/2 teaspoon salt
1 cup chopped walnuts
1/2 cup chocolate chips

Directions:
Pour eggs, butter, milk and bananas into the bread maker pan and set aside.
Stir together all dry ingredients in a large mixing bowl.
Add dry ingredients to bread maker pan.
Set to Basic setting, medium crust color, and press Start.
Remove bread and place on a cooling rack before serving.

Nutrition Info: Calories: 260, Sodium: 203 mg, Dietary Fiber: 1.6 g, Fat: 11.3 g, Carbs: 35.9 g, Protein: 5.2 g

Light Corn Bread

Servings: 1 Loaf

Cooking Time: 10 Minutes

Ingredients:
12 slice bread (1½ pounds)
¾ cup milk, at 80°F to 90°F
1 egg, at room temperature
2¼ tablespoons butter, melted and cooled
2¼ tablespoons honey
¾ teaspoon salt
⅓ cup cornmeal
2⅔ cups white bread flour
1¾ teaspoons bread machine or instant yeast

Directions:
Preparing the Ingredients.
Choose the size of loaf of your preference and then measure the ingredients.
Add all of the ingredients mentioned previously in the list.
Close the lid after placing the pan in the bread machine.
Select the Bake cycle
Turn on the bread machine. Select the White/Basic setting, select the loaf size, and the crust color. Press start.
When the cycle is finished, carefully remove the pan from the bread maker and let it rest.
Remove the bread from the pan, put in a wire rack to Cool about 5 minutes. Slice

Nutrition Info: Calories168, Carbohydrates: 31g, Fat: 4g, Protein: 6g

Potato Honey Bread

Servings: 1 Loaf

Cooking Time: 10 Minutes

Ingredients:
12 slice bread (1½ pounds)
¾ cup lukewarm water
½ cup finely mashed potatoes, at room temperature
egg, at room temperature
¼ cup unsalted butter, melted
tablespoons honey
1 teaspoon table salt
3 cups white bread flour
2 teaspoons bread machine yeast

Directions:
Preparing the Ingredients.
Choose the size of loaf of your preference and then measure the ingredients.
Add all of the ingredients mentioned previously in the list.
Close the lid after placing the pan in the bread machine.
Select the Bake cycle
Turn on the bread machine. Select the White/Basic setting, select the loaf size, and the crust color. Press start.
When the cycle is finished, carefully remove the pan from the bread maker and let it rest.
Remove the bread from the pan, put in a wire rack to Cool about 10 minutes. Slice

Nutrition Info: Calories: 213, Carbohydrates: 25g, Fat: 4.5g, Protein: 6.4g

Zucchini Bread

Servings: 12 Slices

Cooking Time: 10 Minutes

Ingredients:
1/2 teaspoon salt
1 cup sugar
1 tablespoon pumpkin pie spice
1 tablespoon baking powder
teaspoon pure vanilla extract
1/3 cup milk
1/2 cup vegetable oil
eggs
2 cups bread flour
1 1/2 teaspoons active dry yeast or bread machine yeast
1 cup shredded zucchini, raw and unpeeled
1 cup of chopped walnuts (optional)

Directions:
Preparing the Ingredients
Add all of the ingredients for the zucchini bread into the bread maker pan in the order listed above, reserving yeast.
Make a well in the center of the dry ingredients and add the yeast.
Select the Bake cycle
Select Wheat bread cycle, medium crust color, and press Start.
Transfer to a cooling rack for 10 to 15 minutes before slicing to serve.

Nutrition Info: Calories: 196, Carbohydrates: 35g, Fat: 6g,
Protein: 7.5g

Black Olive Bread

Servings: 1 Loaf

Cooking Time: 10 Minutes

Ingredients:
12 slices (1½ pounds)
1 cup milk, at 80°F to 90°F
1½ tablespoons melted butter, cooled
1 teaspoon minced garlic
1½ tablespoons sugar
1 teaspoon salt
3 cups white bread flour
1 teaspoon bread machine or instant yeast
⅓ cup chopped black olives

Directions:
Preparing the Ingredients.
Choose the size of loaf of your preference and then measure the ingredients.
Add all of the ingredients mentioned previously in the list. Close the lid after placing the pan in the bread machine.
Select the Bake cycle
Turn on the bread machine. Select the White/Basic setting, select the loaf size, and the crust color. Press start.
When the cycle is finished, carefully remove the pan from the bread maker and let it rest.
Remove the bread from the pan, put in a wire rack to cool for at least 10 minutes.

Nutrition Info: Calories: 151, Carbohydrates: 29g, Fat: 4g, Protein: 6g

Raisin Candied Fruit Bread

Servings: 1 Loaf

Cooking Time: 10 Minutes

Ingredients:
16 slice bread (2 pounds)
egg, beaten
1½ cups + 1 tablespoon lukewarm water
⅔ teaspoon ground cardamom
1¼ teaspoons table salt
tablespoons sugar
⅓ cup butter, melted
4 cups bread flour
1¼ teaspoons bread machine yeast
½ cup raisins
½ cup mixed candied fruit

Directions:
Preparing the Ingredients.
Choose the size of loaf of your preference and then measure the ingredients.
Add all of the ingredients mentioned previously in the list, except for the candied fruits and raisins. Close the lid after placing the pan in the bread machine.
Select the Bake cycle
Turn on the bread machine. White/Basic or Fruit/Nut (if your machine has this setting) setting, select the loaf size, and the crust color. Press start.
When the machine signals to add ingredients, add the candied fruits and raisins. When the cycle is finished, carefully remove the pan from the bread maker and let it rest.
Remove the bread from the pan, put in a wire rack to cool for at least 10 minutes, and slice.

Nutrition Info: Calories: 184, Carbohydrates: 34g, Fat: 6.3g, Protein: 7g

Blueberry Honey Bread

Servings: 1 Loaf

Cooking Time: 10 Minutes

Ingredients:
16 slice bread (2 pounds)
1 cup plain yogurt
⅔ cup lukewarm water
¼ cup honey
4 teaspoons unsalted butter, melted
2 teaspoons table salt
1½ teaspoons lime zest
⅔ teaspoon lemon extract
4 cups white bread flour
2¼ teaspoons bread machine yeast
1⅓ cups dried blueberries

Directions:
Preparing the Ingredients.
Choose the size of loaf of your preference and then measure the ingredients.
Add all of the ingredients mentioned previously in the list, except for the blueberries. Close the lid after placing the pan in the bread machine.
Select the Bake cycle
Turn on the bread machine. White/Basic or Fruit/Nut (if your machine has this setting) setting, select the loaf size, and the crust color. Press start.
When the machine signals to add ingredients, add the blueberries. When the cycle is finished, carefully remove the pan from the bread maker and let it rest. 8.   Remove the bread from the pan, put in a wire rack to cool for at least 10 minutes, and slice.

Nutrition Info: Calories: 166, Carbohydrates: 38g, Fat: 5.3g, Protein: 6.5g

Carrot Coriander Bread

Servings: 14 Slices

Cooking Time: 3 H.

Ingredients:
2-3 freshly grated carrots,
1⅛ cup lukewarm water
2 Tbsp sunflower oil
4 tsp freshly chopped coriander
2½ cups unbleached white bread flour
2 tsp ground coriander
1 tsp salt
5 tsp sugar
4 tsp easy blend dried yeast

Directions:
Add each ingredient to the bread machine in the order and at the temperature recommended by your bread machine manufacturer. Close the lid, select the basic bread, medium crust setting on your bread machine, and press start.
When the bread machine has finished baking, remove the bread and put it on a cooling.

Nutrition Info: Calories: 1656, Carbohydrates: 32g, Fat: 5.1g, Protein: 6.3g

Brown Bread With Raisins

Servings: 1 Loaf

Cooking Time: 10 Minutes

Ingredients:
32 slices
1 cup all-purpose flour
1 cup whole wheat flour
1 cup whole-grain cornmeal
cup raisins
cups buttermilk
¾ cup molasses
2 teaspoons baking soda
1 teaspoon salt

Directions:
Preparing the Ingredients.
Choose the size of loaf of your preference and then measure the ingredients.
Add all of the ingredients mentioned previously in the list. Close the lid after placing the pan in the bread machine.
Select the Bake cycle
Turn on the bread machine. Select the White/Basic setting, select the loaf size, and the crust color. Press start.
When the cycle is finished, carefully remove the pan from the bread maker and let it rest.
Remove the bread from the pan, put in a wire rack to Cool completely, about 30 minutes.

Nutrition Info: Calories: 136, Carbohydrates: 28g, Fat: 4.3g, Protein: 5.5g

Blueberries 'n Orange Bread

Servings: 1 Loaf

Cooking Time: 10 Minutes

Ingredients:
18 slices bread
3 cups Original Bisquick mix
½ cup granulated sugar
1 tablespoon grated orange peel
½ cup milk
3 tablespoons vegetable oil
2 eggs
1 cup fresh or frozen (rinsed and drained) blueberries glaze
½ cup powdered sugar
3 to 4 teaspoons orange juice
Additional grated orange peel, if desired

Directions:
Preparing the Ingredients.
Choose the size of loaf of your preference and then measure the ingredients.
Add all of the ingredients mentioned previously in the list. Close the lid after placing the pan in the bread machine.
Select the Bake cycle
Program the machine for Basic/White bread, select light or medium crust, and press Start. When the loaf is done, remove the bucket from the machine. Let the loaf cool for 5 minutes.
Gently shake the bucket to remove the loaf, and turn it out onto a rack to cool. Cool completely, about 45 minutes.
In small bowl, mix powdered sugar and orange juice until smooth and thin enough to drizzle. Drizzle glaze over bread; sprinkle with additional orange peel.

Nutrition Info: Calories: 156, Carbohydrates: 6g, Protein: 7g, Fat: 13g

French Onion Bread

Servings: 1 Loaf

Cooking Time: 10 Minutes

Ingredients:
12 slice bread (1½ pounds)
1¼ cups milk, at 80°F to 90°F
¼ cup melted butter, cooled
3 tablespoons light brown sugar
1 teaspoon salt
3 tablespoons dehydrated onion flakes
2 tablespoons chopped fresh chives
1 teaspoon garlic powder
3 cups white bread flour
1 teaspoon bread machine or instant yeast

Directions:
Preparing the Ingredients.
Choose the size of loaf of your preference and then measure the ingredients.
Add all of the ingredients mentioned previously in the list.
Close the lid after placing the pan in the bread machine.
Select the Bake cycle
Turn on the bread machine. Select the White/Basic setting, select the loaf size, and the crust color. Press start.
When the cycle is finished, carefully remove the pan from the bread maker and let it rest.
Remove the bread from the pan, put in a wire rack to Cool about 5 minutes. Slice

Nutrition Info: Calories: 114, Carbohydrates: 6g, Protein: 8g, Fat: 12g

Fresh Blueberry Bread

Servings: 1 Loaf

Cooking Time: 10 Minutes

Ingredients:
12 to 16 slices (1½ to 2 pounds)
1 cup plain Greek yogurt, at room temperature
½ cup milk, at room temperature
3 tablespoons butter, at room temperature
2 eggs, at room temperature
½ cup sugar
¼ cup light brown sugar
teaspoon pure vanilla extract
½ teaspoon lemon zest
cups all-purpose flour
1 tablespoon baking powder
¾ teaspoon salt
¼ teaspoon ground nutmeg
1 cup blueberries

Directions:
Preparing the Ingredients.
Place the yogurt, milk, butter, eggs, sugar, brown sugar, vanilla, and zest in your bread machine.
Select the Bake cycle.
Program the machine for Quick/Rapid bread and press Start. While the wet ingredients are mixing, stir together the flour, baking powder, salt, and nutmeg in a medium bowl. After the first fast mixing is done and the machine signals, add the dry ingredients. When the second mixing cycle is complete, stir in the blueberries. When the loaf is done, remove the bucket from the machine. Let the loaf cool for 5 minutes. Gently shake the bucket to remove the loaf, and turn it out onto a rack to cool.

Nutrition Info: Calories: 176, Carbohydrates: 8g, Protein: 7g, Fat: 14g

Ginger-carrot-nut Bread

Servings: 1 Loaf

Cooking Time: 10 Minutes

Ingredients:
2 eggs
¾ cup packed brown sugar
1/3 cup vegetable oil
½ cup milk
teaspoon vanilla
cups all-purpose flour
2 teaspoons baking powder
1 teaspoon ground ginger
½ teaspoon salt
1 cup shredded carrots (2 medium)
½ cup chopped nuts

Directions:
Preparing the Ingredients.
Choose the size of loaf of your preference and then measure the ingredients.
Add all of the ingredients mentioned previously in the list. Close the lid after placing the pan in the bread machine
Select the Bake cycle
Turn on the bread machine. Select the White/Basic setting, select the loaf size, and the crust color. Press start.
When the cycle is finished, carefully remove the pan from the bread maker and let it rest. 7. Remove the bread from the pan, put in a wire rack to cool. Cool completely, about 10 minutes. Wrap tightly and store at room temperature up to 4 days, or refrigerate.

Nutrition Info: Calories: 122, Carbohydrates: 3g, Protein: 8g, Fat: 13g

Apple-fig Bread With Honey Glaze

Servings: 1 Loaf

Cooking Time: 10 Minutes

Ingredients:
1½ cups all-purpose flour
1½ teaspoons ground cinnamon
1 teaspoon baking powder
½ teaspoon salt
½ teaspoon ground nutmeg
¼ teaspoon ground allspice
2/3 cup granulated sugar
½ cup vegetable oil
1 egg
1 egg yolk
1½ teaspoons vanilla
½ cup milk
cup chopped peeled apples
½ cup dried figs, chopped glaze
1/3 to ½ cup powdered sugar
tablespoons honey
1 tablespoon butter, softened
Dash ground allspice

Directions:
Preparing the Ingredients.
Choose the size of loaf of your preference and then measure the ingredients.
Add all of the ingredients mentioned previously in the list. Close the lid after placing the pan in the bread machine
Select the Bake cycle
Turn on the bread machine. Select the White/Basic setting, select the loaf size, and the crust color. Press start.
When the cycle is finished, carefully remove the pan from the bread maker and let it rest. Remove the bread from the pan, put in a wire rack to cool. Cool completely, about 2 hours. In small bowl, beat 1/3 cup powdered sugar, the honey, butter and dash of allspice until smooth, slowly adding additional powdered sugar for desired glaze consistency. Spread glaze over top of loaf. Let stand until set. (Glaze will remain slightly tacky to the touch.) Wrap tightly and store in refrigerator.

Nutrition Info: Calories: 131, Carbohydrates: 4.9g, Protein: 7.5g, Fat: 15g

Chai-spiced Bread

Servings: 1 Loaf

Cooking Time: 10 Minutes

Ingredients:
¾ cup granulated sugar
½ cup butter, softened
½ cup cold brewed tea or water
1/3 cup milk
2 teaspoons vanilla
2 eggs
2 cups all-purpose flour
2 teaspoons baking powder
¾ teaspoon ground cardamom
½ teaspoon salt
¼ teaspoon ground cinnamon
1/8 teaspoon ground cloves
glaze
1 cup powdered sugar
¼ teaspoon vanilla
3 to 5 teaspoons milk
Additional ground cinnamon

Directions:
Preparing the Ingredients.
Choose the size of loaf of your preference and then measure the ingredients. Add all of the ingredients mentioned previously in the list. Close the lid after placing the pan in the bread machine.
Select the Bake cycle
Turn on the bread machine. Select the White/Basic setting, select the loaf size, and the crust color. Press start.
When the cycle is finished, carefully remove the pan from the bread maker and let it rest. Remove the bread from the pan, put in a wire rack to cool for at least 2 hours, and slice.
Wrap tightly and store at room temperature up to 4 days, or refrigerate.

Nutrition Info: Calories: 121, Carbohydrates: 4g, Protein: 7g, Fat: 16g

Harvest Fruit Bread

Servings: 14 Slices

Cooking Time: 3 H.

Ingredients:
1 cup plus 2 Tbsp water (70°F to 80°F)
1 egg
3 Tbsp butter, softened
¼ cup packed brown sugar
1½ tsp salt
¼ tsp ground nutmeg
Dash allspice
3¾ cups plus 1 Tbsp bread flour
2 tsp active dry yeast
1 cup dried fruit (dried cherries, cranberries and/or raisins)
⅓ cup chopped pecans

Directions:
Add each ingredient except the fruit and pecans to the bread machine in the order and at the temperature recommended by your bread machine manufacturer.
Close the lid, select the basic bread, medium crust setting on your bread machine, and press start.
Just before the final kneading, add the fruit and pecans.
When the bread machine has finished baking, remove the bread and put it on a cooling rack.

Nutrition Info: Calories: 134, Carbohydrates: 6g, Protein: 7g, Fat: 18g

Blueberry-basil Loaf

Servings: 1 Loaf

Cooking Time: 10 Minutes

Ingredients:
12 slice bread (1½ pounds)
1¼ cups fresh blueberries
1 tablespoon all-purpose flour
2¼ cups all-purpose flour
cup granulated sugar
teaspoons baking powder
1 teaspoon grated lemon peel
½ teaspoon salt
1 cup buttermilk
6 tablespoons butter, melted
teaspoon vanilla
eggs
¼ cup coarsely chopped fresh basil leaves
Topping
½ cup packed brown sugar
¼ cup butter, melted
2/3 cup all-purpose flour

Directions:
Preparing the Ingredients.
Choose the size of loaf of your preference and then measure the ingredients.
Add all of the ingredients mentioned previously in the list. Close the lid after placing the pan in the bread machine.
Select the Bake cycle
Turn on the bread machine. Select the White/Basic setting, select the loaf size, and the crust color. Press start.
When the cycle is finished, carefully remove the pan from the bread maker and let it rest.
Remove the bread from the pan, put in a wire rack to Cool about 1 hour

CLASSIC DAILY BREAD

Oat Quinoa Bread

Servings: 1 Loaf

Ingredients:
16 slice bread (2 pounds)
1⅓ cups lukewarm milk
¾ cup cooked quinoa, cooled
5 tablespoons unsalted butter, melted
4 teaspoons sugar
1⅓ teaspoons table salt
2 cups white bread flour
5 tablespoons quick oats
1 cup whole-wheat flour
2 teaspoons bread machine yeast
12 slice bread (1½ pounds)
1 cup lukewarm milk
⅔ cup cooked quinoa, cooled
¼ cup unsalted butter, melted
1 tablespoon sugar
1 teaspoon table salt
1½ cups white bread flour
¼ cup quick oats
¾ cup whole-wheat flour
1½ teaspoons bread machine yeast

Directions:

Choose the size of loaf you would like to make and measure your ingredients.

Add the ingredients to the bread pan in the order listed above.

Place the pan in the bread machine and close the lid.

Turn on the bread maker. Select the White/Basic setting, then the loaf size, and finally the crust color. Start the cycle.

When the cycle is finished and the bread is baked, carefully remove the pan from the machine. Use a potholder as the handle will be very hot. Let rest for a few minutes.

Remove the bread from the pan and allow to cool on a wire rack for at least 10 minutes before slicing.

Nutrition Info: (Per Serving): Calories 153, fat 5.3g, carbs 22.3g, sodium 238mg, protein 3.8g

Lemon Cake

Servings: 12

Cooking Time: 2 Hours 50 Minutes

Ingredients:
3 large eggs, beaten
1/3 cup 2% milk
1/2 cup butter, melted
cups all-purpose flour
teaspoons baking powder
1 1/3 cup sugar
1 teaspoon vanilla extract
2 lemons, zested
For the glaze:
cup powdered sugar
tablespoons lemon juice, freshly squeezed

Directions:
Prepare the glaze by whisking the powdered sugar and lemon juice together in a small mixing bowl and set aside.
Add all of the remaining ingredients to the baking pan in the order listed.
Select the Sweet bread, medium color crust, and press Start.
When baked, transfer the baking pan to a cooling rack.
When the cake has cooled completely, gently shake the cake out onto a serving plate. Glaze the cool cake and serve.

Nutrition Info: Calories: 290, Sodium: 77mg, Dietary Fiber: 0.6g, Fat: 9.3g, Carbs: 42.9g, Protein: 4g.

Classic Whole Wheat Bread

Servings: 1 Loaf

Ingredients:
16 slice bread (2 pounds)
cup lukewarm water
½ cup unsalted butter, melted
eggs, at room temperature
2 teaspoons table salt
¼ cup sugar
1½ cups whole-wheat flour
2½ cups white bread flour
2¼ teaspoons bread machine yeast
12 slice bread (1½ pounds)
¾ cup lukewarm water
⅓ cup unsalted butter, melted
eggs, at room temperature
1½ teaspoons table salt
tablespoons sugar
cup whole-wheat flour
cups white bread flour
1⅔ teaspoons bread machine yeast

Directions:

Choose the size of loaf you would like to make and measure your ingredients.

Add the ingredients to the bread pan in the order listed above.

Place the pan in the bread machine and close the lid.

Turn on the bread maker. Select the Whole Wheat/ Wholegrain or White/Basic setting, wither one will work well for this recipe. Then select the loaf size, and finally the crust color. Start the cycle.

When the cycle is finished and the bread is baked, carefully remove the pan from the machine. Use a potholder as the handle will be very hot. Let rest for a few minutes.

Remove the bread from the pan and allow to cool on a wire rack for at least 10 minutes before slicing.

Nutrition Info: (Per Serving): Calories 176, fat 5.3g, carbs 24.2g, sodium 294mg, protein 5.2g

Garlic Cheese Pull-apart Rolls

Servings: 12 – 24

Cooking Time: 3 Hours

Ingredients:
1 cup water
3 cups bread flour
1 1/2 teaspoons salt
1-1/2 tablespoons butter
3 tablespoons sugar
2 tablespoons nonfat dry milk powder
2 teaspoons yeast
For the topping:
1/4 cup butter, melted
garlic clove, crushed
tablespoons parmesan cheese, plus more if needed
Flour, for surface

Directions:
Place first 6 ingredients in bread maker pan in order listed.
Make a well in the flour; pour the yeast into the hole.
Select Dough cycle, press Start.
Turn finished dough onto a floured countertop.
Gently roll and stretch dough into a 24-inch rope.
Grease a 13-by-9-inch baking sheet.
Divide dough into 24 pieces with a sharp knife and shape into balls; place on prepared pan. Combine butter and garlic in a small mixing bowl and pour over rolls.
Sprinkle rolls evenly with parmesan cheese.
Cover and let rise for 30-45 minutes until doubled.
Bake at 375°F for 10 to 15 minutes or until golden brown.
Remove from oven, pull apart, and serve warm.

Nutrition Info: Calories: 109, Sodium: 210mg, Dietary Fiber: 0.6g, Fat: 3.5g, Carbs: 16.7g, Protein: 2.6g.

Donuts

Servings: 24

Cooking Time: 55 Minutes

Ingredients:
1 1/4 cups whole milk
1 beaten egg
1/4 cup shortening
1/4 cup sugar
1 teaspoon salt
3 1/2 cups all-purpose flour
1 1/2 teaspoons dry yeast

Directions:
Measure ingredients into the bread maker, first adding wet then dry ingredients as listed above, reserving yeast.
Make a well in the flour; pour the yeast into the hole.
Select Dough cycle and press Start.
Roll kneaded dough out to a 1/2-inch thick rectangle and cut with a 2 1/2 inch donut cutter.
Let rise, covered, for 30 minutes or until doubled in size.
Preheat a deep fryer to 375°F.
Drop donuts into fryer and turn donuts as they rise to the surface. Fry until golden brown.
Drain on paper towels to cool. Glaze or dust with your favorite donut topping while
warm and serve.

Nutrition Info: Calories: 104, Sodium: 105mg, Dietary Fiber: 0.5g, Fat: 3g, Carbs: 16.7g, Protein: 2.7g.

Everything Bagel Loaf

Servings: 6 - 8

Cooking Time: 3 Hours 25 Minutes

Ingredients:
cup plus 3 tablespoons water
tablespoons vegetable oil
1/2 teaspoons salt
tablespoons sugar
1/4 cups white bread flour
3 tablespoons Everything Bagel seasoning
2 teaspoons active dry yeast

Directions:
Add water and oil to the bread maker pan.
Add salt, Everything Bagel seasoning, and sugar.
Add flour.
Make a small well on top of the flour and be sure it does not reach wet ingredients. Add the yeast to the well.
Select Basic bread cycle, medium crust color, and press Start.
When bread is baked, allow the loaf cool on a cooling rack for about 30 minutes before serving.

Nutrition Info: Calories: 44, Sodium: 438mg, Dietary Fiber: 0.2g, Fat: 3.5g, Carbs: 3.4g, Protein: 0.4g.

Peanut Butter Bread

Servings: 10

Cooking Time: 3 Hours And 25 Minutes

Ingredients:
Water – 1 cup, plus 1 tbsp.
Peanut butter – ½ cup
Bread flour – 3 cups
Brown sugar – 3 tbsp.
Salt – 1 tsp.
Bread machine yeast – 2 tsp.

Directions:
Place every ingredient in the bread machine according to the manufacturer's recommendation.
Select Basic/White or Sweet and choose Medium or Light crust. Press Start.
Remove the bread when finished.
Cool, slice, and serve.

Nutrition Info: (Per Serving): Calories: 136, Total Fat: 8g, Saturated Fat: 1g, Carbohydrates: 14g, Cholesterol: 0mg, Fiber: 2 g, Calcium: 32mg, Sodium: 203mg, Protein: 4 g

Pizza Dough

Servings: 12 - 14

Cooking Time: 1 Hour 30 Minutes

Ingredients:
1 1/4 cups water
3 cups bread flour
1 teaspoon milk powder
1 tablespoon sugar
1 teaspoon salt
1 tablespoon yeast

Directions:
Add ingredients to the bread maker pan in the order listed above.
Select Dough cycle and press Start.
When finished, prepare dough by rolling it out in a pizza pan about to
a 1-inch thickness.
Top with your favorite sauce, then cheese, then other toppings like
pepperoni or veggies.
Bake at 425°F for 15 to 20 minutes or until crust is golden on the
edges.
Enjoy hot!

Nutrition Info: Calories: 103, Sodium: 168mg, Dietary Fiber: 0.9g,
Fat: 0.3g, Carbs: 21.7g, Protein: 3.1g

10 Minute Rosemary Bread

Servings: 12

Cooking Time: 2 Hours

Ingredients:
cup warm water, about 105°F
tablespoons butter, softened
1 egg
3 cups all-purpose flour
1/4 cup whole wheat flour
1/3 cup sugar
1 teaspoon salt
3 teaspoons bread maker yeast
2 tablespoons rosemary, freshly chopped For the topping:
1 egg, room temperature
1 teaspoon milk, room temperature
Garlic powder Sea salt

Directions:
Place all of the ingredients in the bread maker pan in the order listed above.
Select Dough cycle.
When dough is kneaded, place on parchment paper on a flat surface and roll into two loaves; set aside and allow to rise for 30 minutes.
Preheat a pizza stone in an oven on 375°F for 30 minutes.
For the topping, add the egg and milk to a small mixing bowl and whisk to create an egg wash. Baste the formed loaves and sprinkle evenly with garlic powder and sea salt.
Allow to rise for 40 minutes, lightly covered, in a warm area.
Bake for 15 to 18 minutes or until golden brown. Serve warm.

Nutrition Info: Calories: 176, Sodium: 220mg, Dietary Fiber: 1.5g, Fat: 3.1g, Carbs: 32g, Protein: 5g

Multigrain Loaf

Servings: 12

Cooking Time: 3 Hours And 25 Minutes

Ingredients:
Water – 1 ¼ cup
Butter – 2 tbsp., softened
Bread flour – 1 1/3 cups
Whole wheat flour – 1 1/3 cup
Multigrain hot cereal – 1 ¼ cups, uncooked
Brown sugar – ¼ cup
Salt – 1 ½ tsp.
Bread machine yeast – 2 ½ tsp.

Directions:
Place all ingredients in the bread machine according to manufacture recommendation.
Select Basic/White cycle and Medium or Light crust. Press Start.
Remove the bread when done.
Cool, slice, and serve.

Nutrition Info: (Per Serving): Calories: 170, Total Fat: 2g, Saturated Fat: 2g, Carbohydrates: 31g, Cholesterol: 5mg, Fiber: 4g, Calcium: 0mg, Sodium: 260mg, Protein: 5g

Flaxseed Milk Bread

Servings: 1 Loaf

Ingredients:
16 slice bread (2 pounds)
1½ cups lukewarm milk
2 tablespoons unsalted butter, melted
2 tablespoons honey
2 teaspoons table salt
4 cups white bread flour
½ cup flaxseed
1½ teaspoons bread machine yeast
12 slice bread (1½ pounds)
1⅛ cups lukewarm milk
1½ tablespoons unsalted butter, melted
1½ tablespoons honey
1 teaspoon table salt
3 cups white bread flour
¼ cup flaxseed
1¼ teaspoons bread machine yeast

Directions:
Choose the size of loaf you would like to make and measure your ingredients.
Add the ingredients to the bread pan in the order listed above.
Place the pan in the bread machine and close the lid.
Turn on the bread maker. Select the White/Basic setting, then the loaf size, and finally the crust color. Start the cycle.
When the cycle is finished and the bread is baked, carefully remove the pan from the machine. Use a potholder as the handle will be very hot.
Let rest for a few minutes.
Remove the bread from the pan and allow to cool on a wire rack for at least 10 minutes before slicing.

Nutrition Info: (Per Serving): Calories 147, fat 3.2g, carbs 27.4g, sodium 216mg, protein 5.8g

Garlic Pepperoni Bread

Servings: 14 Slices

Cooking Time: 3 H.
1 cup water
¼ cup light olive oil
3 cups bread flour
1 Tbsp sugar
1 tsp salt
½-1 tsp garlic powder
½-1 Tbsp minced dried onions
tsp dried basil
¼ cup shredded mozzarella cheese
⅓ cup grated parmesan cheese
¼ cup pepperoni slice, chopped
tsp bread machine yeast

Directions:
Add each ingredient to the bread machine in the order and at the temperature recommended by your bread machine manufacturer. Close the lid, select the basic bread, medium crust setting on your bread machine, and press start.
When the bread machine has finished baking, remove the bread and put it on a cooling rack.

Nutrition Info: Calories: 153, Carbohydrates: 34g, Fat: 3.9g, Protein: 3.5g

Buttermilk Bread

Servings: 1 Loaf

Ingredients:
16 slice bread (2 pounds)
1¼ cups lukewarm buttermilk
2 tablespoons unsalted butter, melted
2 tablespoons sugar
1½ teaspoons table salt
½ teaspoon baking powder
3½ cups white bread flour
2¼ teaspoons bread machine yeast
12 slice bread (1½ pounds)
1¼ cups lukewarm buttermilk
1½ tablespoons unsalted butter, melted
1½ tablespoons sugar
1⅛ teaspoons table salt
⅓ teaspoon baking powder
2⅔ cups white bread flour
1⅔ teaspoons bread machine yeast

Directions:
Choose the size of loaf you would like to make and measure your ingredients.
Add the ingredients to the bread pan in the order listed above.
Place the pan in the bread machine and close the lid.
Turn on the bread maker. Select the White/Basic setting, then the loaf size, and finally the crust color. Start the cycle.
When the cycle is finished and the bread is baked, carefully remove the pan from the machine. Use a potholder as the handle will be very hot. Let rest for a few minutes. 6   Remove the bread from the pan and allow to cool on a wire rack for at least 10 minutes before slicing.

Nutrition Info: (Per Serving): Calories 132, fat 2.2g, carbs 23.4g, sodium 234mg, protein 4.3g

Coffee Rye Bread

Servings: 6

Cooking Time: 3 Hours And 25 Minutes

Ingredients:
Lukewarm water – ½ cup
Brewed coffee – ¼ cup, 80°F
Dark molasses – 2 tbsp.
Brown sugar – 5 tsp.
Unsalted butter – 4 tsp., softened
Powdered skim milk – 1 tbsp.
Kosher salt – 1 tsp.
Unsweetened cocoa powder – 4 tsp.
Dark rye flour – 2/3 cup
Whole-wheat bread machine flour – ½ cup
Caraway seeds – 1 tsp.
White bread machine flour – 1 cup
Bread machine yeast – 1 ½ tsp

Directions:
Place everything in the bread machine pan according to the bread
machine recommendation.
Select Basic and Light crust. Press Start.
Remove the bread.
Cool, slice, and serve.

Nutrition Info: (Per Serving): Calories: 222, Total Fat: 3.2g, Saturated
Fat: 1.8 g, Carbohydrates: 42.9 g, Cholesterol: 8 mg, Fiber: 4.7 g,
Calcium: 40 mg, Sodium: 415 mg, Protein: 6.3 g

Apple Walnut Bread

Servings: 14 Slices

Cooking Time: 2 H. 30 Min.

Ingredients:
¾ cup unsweetened applesauce
4 cups apple juice
1 tsp salt
3 Tbsp butter
1 large egg
4 cups bread flour
¼ cup brown sugar, packed
1¼ tsp cinnamon
½ tsp baking soda
2 tsp active dry yeast
½ cup chopped walnuts
½ cup chopped dried cranberries

Directions:
Add each ingredient to the bread machine in the order and at the temperature recommended by your bread machine manufacturer. Close the lid, select the basic bread, medium crust setting on your bread machine, and press start.
When the bread machine has finished baking, remove the bread and put it on a cooling rack.

Nutrition Info: Calories: 146, Carbohydrates: 38g, Fat: 5g, Protein: 4g

Honey Wheat Bread

Servings: 1 Loaf

Ingredients:
16 slice bread (2 pounds)
1⅔ cups boiling water
¼ cup + 4 teaspoons cracked wheat
¼ cup + 4 teaspoons unsalted butter, melted
¼ cup honey
2 teaspoons table salt
1⅓ cups whole-wheat flour
2⅔ cups white bread flour
2½ teaspoons bread machine yeast
12 slice bread (1½ pounds)
1¼ cups boiling water
¼ cup cracked wheat
¼ cup unsalted butter, melted
3 tablespoons honey
1½ teaspoons table salt
cup whole-wheat flour
cups white bread flour
2 teaspoons bread machine yeast

Directions:

Choose the size of loaf you would like to make and measure your ingredients.

Add the boiling water and cracked wheat to the bread pan; set aside for 25–30 minutes for the wheat to soften.

Add the other ingredients to the bread pan in the order listed above.

Place the pan in the bread machine and close the lid.

Turn on the bread maker. Select the White/Basic setting, then the loaf size, and finally

the crust color. Start the cycle.

When the cycle is finished and the bread is baked, carefully remove the pan from the machine. Use a potholder as the handle will be very hot.

Let rest for a few minutes.

Remove the bread from the pan and allow to cool on a wire rack for at least 10 minutes before slicing.

Nutrition Info: (Per Serving): Calories 168, fat 4.3g, carbs 31.3g, sodium 296mg, protein 4.1g

Chocolate Chip Bread

Servings: 14 Slices

Cooking Time: 3 H.

Ingredients:
¼ cup water
1 cup milk
1 egg
3 cups bread flour
3 Tbsp brown sugar
2 Tbsp white sugar
1 tsp salt
tsp ground cinnamon
1½ tsp active dry yeast
Tbsp margarine, softened
¾ cup semisweet chocolate chips

Directions:
Add each ingredient except the chocolate chips to the bread machine in the order and at the temperature recommended by your bread machine manufacturer.
Close the lid, select the sweet loaf, low crust setting on your bread machine, and press start.
Add the chocolate chips about 5 minutes before the kneading cycle has finished.
When the bread machine has finished baking, remove the bread and put it on a cooling rack.

Nutrition Info: Calories: 136, Carbohydrates: 32g, Fat: 7.3g, Protein: 8.5g

Sausage Herb And Onion Bread

Servings: 14 Slices

Cooking Time: 3 H. 10 Min.
¾ tsp basil leaves
1½ Tbsp sugar
⅜ cup wheat bran
1 medium onion, minced
2¼ tsp yeast
¾ tsp rosemary leaves
½ Tbsp salt
1½ Tbsp parmesan, grated
3 cups bread flour
¾ tsp oregano leaves
¾ tsp thyme leaves
1⅛ cups water
¾ cup Italian sausage

Directions:
Remove casing from sausage. Crumble the meat into a medium nonstick skillet.
Cook on medium heat, stirring and breaking up sausage until it begins to render its juices.
Add onion and cook for 2-3 minuts until it softens and the sausage is no longer pink.
Remove from heat and let it cool.
Add each ingredient to the bread machine in the order and at the temperature recommended by your bread machine manufacturer.
Close the lid, select the basic bread, medium crust setting on your bread machine, and press start.
When the bread machine has finished baking, remove the bread and put it on a cooling rack.

Nutrition Info: Calories: 116, Carbohydrates: 28g, Fat: 3.3g, Protein: 4.5g

Carrot Cake Bread

Servings: 12 - 16

Cooking Time: 1 Hours 20 Minutes

Ingredients:
Non-stick cooking spray
1/4 cup vegetable oil
2 large eggs, room temperature
1/2 teaspoon pure vanilla extract
1/2 cup sugar
1/4 cup light brown sugar
1/4 cup crushed pineapple with juice (from can or fresh)
1 1/4 cups unbleached, all-purpose flour
1 teaspoon baking powder
1/4 teaspoon baking soda
1/4 teaspoon salt
1 teaspoon ground cloves
3/4 teaspoon ground cinnamon
1 cup freshly grated carrots
1/3 cup chopped pecans
1/3 cup golden raisins

Directions:
Coat the inside of the bread pan with non-stick cooking spray.
Add all of the ingredients, in order listed, to the bread pan.
Select Express Bake, medium crust color, and press Start. While the batter is mixing, scrape the sides of the bread pan with a rubber spatula to fully incorporate ingredients.
When baked, remove from bread pan and place on wire rack to cool completely before slicing and serving.

Nutrition Info: Calories: 151, Sodium: 69mg, Dietary Fiber: 1.2g, Fat: 7.2g, Carbs: 20.1g, Protein: 2.4g.

Texas Roadhouse Rolls

Servings: 18 Rolls

Cooking Time: 20 Min.

Ingredients:
¼ cup warm water (80°F - 90°F
1 cup warm milk (80°F -90°F)
1 tsp salt
1½ Tbsp butter + more for brushing
1 egg
¼ cup sugar
3½ cups unbleached bread flour
1 envelope dry active yeast
For Texas roadhouse cinnamon butter:
½ cup sweet, creamy salted butter, softened
⅓ cup confectioners' sugar
1 tsp ground cinnamon

Directions:
Add each ingredient to the bread machine in the order and at the temperature recommended by your bread machine manufacturer.
Select the dough cycle and press start.
Once cycle is done, transfer your dough onto a lightly floured surface.
Roll out the rectangle, fold it in half. Let it rest for 15 minutes.
Cut the roll into 18 squares. Transfer them onto a baking sheet.
Bake at 350°F in a preheated oven for 10-15 minutes.
Remove dough from the oven and brush the top with butter.
Beat the softened butter with a mixer to make it fluffy. Gradually add the sugar and cinnamon while blending. Mix well.
Take out the rolls, let them cool for 2-3 minutes.
Spread them with cinnamon butter on the top while they are warm.

Nutrition Info: Calories: 166, Carbohydrates: 38g, Fat: 5.3g, Protein: 6.5g

Pizza Rolls

Servings: 15

Cooking Time: 3 Hours

Ingredients:
1 cup warm water
3 tablespoons olive oil
3 cups bread flour
3 tablespoons sugar
1/2 teaspoons salt
1/4 teaspoons instant yeast
For the Filling:
1 package pepperoni, sliced
1 bag mozzarella cheese, shredded
1 cup pizza sauce
1 jar of mild banana pepper rings

Directions:
Add the liquid ingredients to your bread maker first, then add flour and salt. Create a small hole in the flour and add the sugar and yeast. Select the Dough cycle and press Start. Once your dough has fully risen, lay it out on a lightly floured surface, and punch it back down. Knead by hand for about 30 seconds; be sure not to overwork the dough. Pinch off a small amount of dough and flatten out into the shape of a circle and baste with one teaspoon of sauce. Layer with three slices of pepperoni, a good pinch of cheese, and a few banana pepper rings. Fold one side over to the other and pinch the seams together, creating a seal. Fold corners over and do the same; repeat until all dough is used.
Place rolls on a large 9-by-13-inch baking sheet and bake at 350°F for about 25 mins or until slightly golden brown.
Remove rolls and allow to cool on a cooling rack for 10 to 15 minutes before eating; serve warm.

Nutrition Info: Calories: 142, Sodium: 329mg, Dietary Fiber: 1.1g, Fat: 3.7g, Carbs: 23.7g, Protein: 3.7g.

Panettone

Servings: 14 Slices

Cooking Time: 3 H. 10 Min.

Ingredients:
¾ cup warm water
6 Tbsp vegetable oil
1½ tsp salt
4 Tbsp sugar
eggs
cups bread flour
1 (¼ ounce) package Fleishman's yeast
½ cup candied fruit
⅓ cup chopped almonds
½ tsp almond extract

Directions:
Add each ingredient to the bread machine in the order and at the temperature recommended by your bread machine manufacturer. Close the lid, select the sweet loaf, low crust setting on your bread machine, and press start.
When the bread machine has finished baking, remove the bread and put it on a cooling rack.

Nutrition Info: Calories: 137, Carbohydrates: 28g, Fat: 3.3g, Protein: 4.5g

Honey Whole Wheat Bread

Servings: 10

Cooking Time: 1 Hour And 20 Minutes

Ingredients:
Warm water - 1 cup
Butter - 2 tbsp., cubed
Salt – 1 tsp.
Honey – 2 tbsp.
Unbleached flour – 1 ½ cups
Whole wheat flour – 1 ½ cups
Bread machine yeast – 2 tsp.

Directions:
Add ingredients according to bread machine instructions.
Select Rapid – Whole Wheat and Medium crust.
Remove bread when done.
Cool and slice.

Nutrition Info: (Per Serving): Calories: 165, Total Fat: 3g,
Saturated Fat: 2g, Carbohydrates: 31g, Cholesterol: 6mg, Fiber: 3g,
Calcium: 25mg, Sodium: 253mg, Protein: 5g

Chocolate Marble Cake

Servings: 12 - 16

Cooking Time: 3 Hours 45 Minutes

Ingredients:
1 1/2 cups water
1 1/2 teaspoons vanilla extract
1 1/2 teaspoons salt
3 1/2 cups bread flour
1 1/2 teaspoons instant yeast
1 cup semi-sweet chocolate chips

Directions:
Set the chocolate chips aside and add the other ingredients to the pan of your bread maker.
Program the machine for Sweet bread and press Start.
Check the dough after 10 to 15 minutes of kneading; you should have a smooth ball, soft but not sticky.
Add the chocolate chips about 3 minutes before the end of the second kneading cycle.
Once baked, remove with a rubber spatula and allow to cool on a rack before serving.

Nutrition Info: Calories: 172, Sodium: 218mg, Dietary Fiber: 1.6g, Fat: 4.3g, Carbs: 30.1g, Protein: 3g.

Chocolate Coffee Bread

Servings: 14 Slices

Cooking Time: 3 H.

Ingredients:
1⅓ cups water
⅓ cup cocoa powder
1⅓ cups bread flour
1⅓ cups whole wheat flour
3 Tbsp powdered milk
½ tsp salt
1½ Tbsp honey
2 envelopes instant mocha cappuccino mix
2¼ tsp active dry yeast
½ cup semi-sweet chocolate chips

Directions:
Add each ingredient except chips and mocha mix to the bread machine in the order and at the temperature recommended by your bread machine manufacturer.
Close the lid, select the sweet loaf, low crust setting on your bread machine, and press start.
Add the chocolate chips and mocha mix about 5 minutes before the kneading cycle has finished.
When the bread machine has finished baking, remove the bread and put it on a cooling rack.

Nutrition Info: Calories: 144, Carbohydrates: 5g, Protein: 6g, Fat: 16g

Classic White Bread

Servings: 1 Loaf

Ingredients:
16 slice bread (2 pounds)
1 1/2 cups water, lukewarm between 80 and 90ºF
3 tablespoons unsalted butter, melted
1 tablespoon sugar
3 tablespoons dry milk powder
1 1/4 teaspoons table salt
4 cup white bread flour
1 1/2 teaspoons bread machine yeast
12 slice bread (1 ½ pounds)
1/4 cups water, lukewarm between 80 and 90ºF
tablespoons unsalted butter, melted
2 teaspoons sugar
2 tablespoons dry milk powder
1 teaspoons table salt
3 1/4 cup white bread flour
1 1/4 teaspoons bread machine yeast

Directions:
Choose the size of loaf you would like to make and measure your ingredients.
Add the ingredients to the bread pan in the order listed above.
Place the pan in the bread machine and close the lid.
Turn on the bread maker. Select the White/Basic setting, then the loaf size, and finally the crust color. Start the cycle.
When the cycle is finished and the bread is baked, carefully remove the pan from the machine. Use a potholder as the handle will be very hot. Let rest for a few minutes.
Remove the bread from the pan and allow to cool on a wire rack for at least 10 minutes before slicing.

Nutrition Info: (Per Serving): Calories 148, fat 3.6g, carbs 23.4g, sodium 197mg, protein 3.4g

Insane Coffee Cake

Servings: 10 - 12

Cooking Time: 2 Hours

Ingredients:
7/8 cup of milk
1/4 cup of sugar
1 teaspoon salt
1 egg yolk
tablespoon butter
1/4 cups bread flour
2 teaspoons of active dry yeast
For the topping:
2 tablespoons butter, melted
2 tablespoons brown sugar
1 teaspoon cinnamon

Directions:
Set the topping ingredients aside and add the rest of the ingredients to the bread pan in the order above.
Set the bread machine to the Dough cycle.
Butter a 9-by-9-inch glass baking dish and pour the dough into the dish. Cover with a towel and let rise for about 10 minutes.
Preheat an oven to 375°F.
Brush the dough with the melted butter.
Mix the brown sugar and cinnamon in a bowl and sprinkle on top of the coffee cake.
Let the topped dough rise, uncovered, for another 30 minutes.
Place in oven and bake for 30 to 35 minutes or until a wooden toothpick inserted into the center comes out clean and dry.
When baked, let the coffee cake rest for 10 minutes. Carefully remove the coffee cake from the dish with a rubber spatula, slice and serve.

Nutrition Info: Calories: 148, Sodium: 211mg, Dietary Fiber: 0.9g, Fat: 3.9g, Carbs: 24.9g, Protein: 3.5g.

Multigrain Honey Bread

Servings: 1 Loaf

Ingredients:
16 slice bread (2 pounds)
1½ cups lukewarm water
2 tablespoons unsalted butter, melted
1 tablespoon honey
teaspoon table salt
1½ cups multigrain flour
2¾ cups white bread flour
teaspoons bread machine yeast
12 slice bread (1½ pounds)
1⅛ cups lukewarm water
2 tablespoons unsalted butter, melted
1½ tablespoons honey
1½ teaspoons table salt
1⅛ cups multigrain flour
2 cups white bread flour
1½ teaspoons bread machine yeast

Directions:
Choose the size of loaf you would like to make and measure your ingredients.
Add the ingredients to the bread pan in the order listed above.
Place the pan in the bread machine and close the lid.
Turn on the bread maker. Select the White/Basic setting, then the loaf size, and finally the crust color. Start the cycle.
When the cycle is finished and the bread is baked, carefully remove the pan from the
machine. Use a potholder as the handle will be very hot. Let rest for a few minutes.
Remove the bread from the pan and allow to cool on a wire rack for at least 10 minutes before slicing.

Nutrition Info: (Per Serving): Calories 144, fat 2.2g, carbs 26.3g, sodium 287mg, protein 4.1g

Golden Turmeric Cardamom Bread

Servings: 12

Cooking Time: 3 Hours

Ingredients:
1 cup lukewarm water
1/3 cup lukewarm milk
3 tablespoons butter, unsalted
3 3/4 cups unbleached all-purpose flour
3 tablespoons sugar
1/2 teaspoons salt
tablespoons ground turmeric
1 tablespoon ground cardamom
1/2 teaspoon cayenne pepper
1 1/2 teaspoons active dry yeast

Directions:
Add liquid ingredients to the bread pan.
Measure and add dry ingredients (except yeast) to the bread pan.
Make a well in the center of the dry ingredients and add the yeast.
Snap the baking pan into the bread maker and close the lid.
Choose the Basic setting, preferred crust color and press Start.
When the loaf is done, remove the pan from the machine. After about 5 minutes, gently shake the pan to loosen the loaf and turn it out onto a rack to cool.

Nutrition Info: Calories: 183, Sodium: 316mg, Dietary Fiber: 1.2g, Fat: 3.3g, Carbs: 33.3g, Protein: 4.5g

Cinnamon Pecan Coffee Cake

Servings: 10 - 12

Cooking Time: 2 Hours

Ingredients:
1 cup butter, unsalted
cup sugar
eggs
1 cup sour cream
teaspoon vanilla extract
cups all-purpose flour
1 teaspoon baking powder
1 teaspoon baking soda
1/2 teaspoon salt
For the topping:
1/2 cup brown sugar
1/4 cup sugar
1/2 teaspoon cinnamon
1/2 cup pecans, chopped

Directions:
Add butter, sugar, eggs, sour cream and vanilla to the bread maker
baking pan, followed by the dry ingredients.
Select Cake cycle and press Start.
Prepare topping and set aside.
When kneading cycle is done, after about 20 minutes, sprinkle 1/2 cup
of topping on top of dough and continue baking.
During the last hour of baking time, sprinkle the remaining 1/2 cup of
topping on the cake. Bake until complete. Cool on a wire rack for 10
minutes and serve warm.

Nutrition Info: Calories: 488, Sodium: 333mg, Dietary Fiber: 2.5g,
Fat: 32.8g, Carbs: 46.4g, Protein: 5.7g.

Oat Bran Molasses Bread

Servings: 8

Cooking Time: 3 Hours And 48 Minutes

Ingredients:
Water - ½ cup
Melted butter - 1½ tbsp., cooled
Blackstrap molasses - 2 tbsp.
Salt - ¼ tsp.
Ground nutmeg - ⅛ tsp.
Oat bran - ½ cup
Whole-wheat bread flour - 1½ cups
Bread machine or instant yeast - 1⅛ tsp.

Directions:
Place the ingredients in the bread machine according to instructions.
Choose Whole-Wheat/Whole-Grain bread, and Light or Medium
crust. Press Start.
Remove when done and cool. Slice and serve.

Nutrition Info: (Per Serving): Calories: 137, Total Fat: 3g,
Saturated Fat: 2g, Carbohydrates: 25g, Cholesterol: 15mg, Fiber: 1g,
Calcium: 20mg, Sodium: 112mg, Protein: 3g

SPICE, NUT & HERB BREAD

Seed Bread

Servings: 1 Loaf

Cooking Time: 10 Minutes

Ingredients:
3 Tbsp flax seed
1 Tbsp sesame seeds
1 Tbsp poppy seeds
¾ cup water
1 Tbsp honey
1 Tbsp canola oil
½ tsp salt
1½ cups bread flour
5 Tbsp wholemeal flour
1¼ tsp dried active baking yeast

Directions:
Preparing the Ingredients
Add each ingredient to the bread machine in the order and at the temperature recommended by your bread machine manufacturer.
Select the Bake cycle
Close the lid, select the basic bread, medium crust setting on your bread machine, and press start.
When the bread machine has finished baking, remove the bread and put it on a cooling rack.

Nutrition Info: Calories: 113, Sodium: 188mg, Dietary Fiber: 0.8g, Fat: 0.4g, Carbs: 23.7g, Protein: 3.3g.

Hazelnut Honey Bread

Servings: 1 Loaf

Cooking Time: 10 Minutes

Ingredients:
16 slices bread (2 pounds)
1⅓ cups lukewarm milk
2 eggs, at room temperature
5 tablespoons unsalted butter, melted
¼ cup honey
1 teaspoon pure vanilla extract
1 teaspoon table salt
4 cups white bread flour
cup toasted hazelnuts, finely ground
teaspoons bread machine yeast

Directions:
Preparing the Ingredients.
Choose the size of loaf of your preference and then measure the ingredients.
Add all of the ingredients mentioned previously in the list.
Close the lid after placing the pan in the bread machine.
Select the Bake cycle
Turn on the bread machine. Select the White/Basic setting, select the loaf size, and the crust color. Press start.
When the cycle is finished, carefully remove the pan from the bread maker and let it rest.
Remove the bread from the pan, put in a wire rack to Cool about 10 minutes. Slice

Nutrition Info: Calories: 133, Sodium: 148mg, Dietary Fiber: g, 1.2 Fat: 0.1g, Carbs: 24.7g, Protein: 3.5g.

Flaxseed Honey Bread

Servings: 1 Loaf

Cooking Time: 10 Minutes

Ingredients:
12 slices bread (1½ pounds)
1⅛ cups milk, at 80°F to 90°F
1½ tablespoons melted butter, cooled
1½ tablespoons honey
1 teaspoon salt
¼ cup flaxseed
3 cups white bread flour
1¼ teaspoons bread machine or instant yeast

Directions:
Preparing the Ingredients.
Choose the size of loaf of your preference and then measure the ingredients.
Add all of the ingredients mentioned previously in the list.
Close the lid after placing the pan in the bread machine.
Select the Bake cycle.
Turn on the bread machine. Select the White/Basic setting, select the loaf size, and the crust color. Press start.
When the cycle is finished, carefully remove the pan from the bread maker and let it rest.
Remove the bread from the pan, put in a wire rack to Cool about 5 minutes. Slice

Nutrition Info: Calories: 133, Sodium: 178mg, Dietary Fiber: 1.3g, Fat: 0.6g, Carbs: 27.7g, Protein: 3.7g.

Healthy Spelt Bread

Servings: 10

Cooking Time: 40 Minutes

Ingredients:
Milk – 1 ¼ cups.
Sugar – 2 tbsps.
Olive oil – 2 tbsps.
Salt – 1 tsp.
Spelt flour – 4 cups.
Yeast – 2 ½ tsps.

Directions:
Add all ingredients to the bread machine pan according to the bread machine manufacturer instructions. Select basic bread setting then select light/medium crust and start. Once loaf is done, remove the loaf pan from the machine. Allow it to cool for 10 minutes. Slice and serve.

Nutrition Info: Calories: 141, Sodium: 138mg, Dietary Fiber: 0.7g, Fat: 0.2g, Carbs: 31.7g, Protein: 2.9g

Quinoa Whole-wheat Bread

Servings: 1 Loaf

Cooking Time: 10 Minutes

Ingredients:
12 slice bread (1½ pounds)
1 cup milk, at 80°F to 90°F
⅔ cup cooked quinoa, cooled
¼ cup melted butter, cooled
1 tablespoon sugar
1 teaspoon salt
¼ cup quick oats
¾ cup whole-wheat flour
1½ cups white bread flour
1½ teaspoons bread machine or instant yeast

Directions:
Preparing the Ingredients.
Choose the size of loaf of your preference and then measure the ingredients.
Add all of the ingredients mentioned previously in the list.
Close the lid after placing the pan in the bread machine.
Select the Bake cycle
Turn on the bread machine. Select the White/Basic setting, select the loaf size, and the crust color. Press start.
When the cycle is finished, carefully remove the pan from the bread maker and let it rest. 8. Remove the bread from the pan, put in a wire rack to Cool about 5 minutes. Slice

Nutrition Info: Calories: 103, Sodium: 168mg, Dietary Fiber: 0.9g, Fat: 0.3g, Carbs: 21.7g, Protein: 3.1g.

Taco Bread

Servings: 20

Cooking Time: 3 Hours And 48 Minutes

Ingredients:
Water - 1 ½ cup
Bread flour – 2 2/3 cups
Whole wheat flour – 2 cups
Sugar – 2 tbsp.
Taco seasoning mix – 3 tbsp.
Salt 1 /2 tsp.
Olive oil – 2 tbsp.
Active dry yeast – 2 tbsp.

Directions:
Add everything according to bread machine recommendation.
Select Whole wheat and Medium crust. Press Start.
Remove the bread when done.
Cool, slice, and serve.

Nutrition Info: (Per Serving): Calories: 127, Total Fat: 1.7g,
Saturated Fat: 0.3 g, Carbohydrates: 24.3 g, Cholesterol: 0mg,
Fiber: 0.9g, Calcium: 5mg, Sodium: 237mg, Protein: 3.2g

Garlic, Herb, And Cheese Bread

Servings: One Loaf (12 Slices)

Cooking Time: 15 Minutes

Ingredients:
1/2 cup ghee
Six eggs
2 cups almond flour
1 tbsp baking powder
1/2 tsp xanthan gum
1 cup cheddar cheese, shredded
1 tbsp garlic powder
1 tbsp parsley
1/2 tbsp oregano
1/2 tsp salt

Directions:
Lightly beat eggs and ghee before pouring into bread machine pan.
Add the remaining ingredients to the pan.
Set bread machine to gluten-free.
When the bread is finished, remove the bread pan from the bread machine.
Let it cool for a while before transferring into a cooling rack.
You can store your bread for up to 5 days in the refrigerator.

Nutrition Info: Calories: 156, Carbohydrates: 4g, Protein: 5g, Fat: 13g

Dilly Onion Bread

Servings: 14 Slices

Cooking Time: 3 H. 5 Min.

Ingredients:
¾ cup water (70°F to 80°F)
Tbsp butter, softened
Tbsp sugar
Tbsp dried minced onion
2 Tbsp dried parsley flakes
1 Tbsp dill weed
1 tsp salt
garlic clove, minced
cups bread flour
⅓ cup whole wheat flour
Tbsp nonfat dry milk powder
tsp active dry yeast serving

Directions:
Add each ingredient to the bread machine in the order and at the
temperature recommended by your bread machine manufacturer.
Close the lid, select the basic bread, medium crust setting on your
bread machine and press start.
When the bread machine has finished baking, remove the bread and
put it on a cooling rack.

Nutrition Info: Calories: 166, Carbohydrates: 4.6g, Protein: 6g,
Fat: 12g

Molasses Candied-ginger Bread

Servings: 1 Loaf

Cooking Time: 10 Minutes

Ingredients:
12 slices bread (1½ pounds)
1 cup milk, at 80°F to 90°F
1 egg, at room temperature
¼ cup dark molasses
3 tablespoons butter, melted and cooled
½ teaspoon salt
¼ cup chopped candied ginger
½ cup quick oats
3 cups white bread flour
2 teaspoons bread machine or instant yeast

Directions:
Preparing the Ingredients.
Choose the size of loaf of your preference and then measure the ingredients.
Add all of the ingredients mentioned previously in the list.
Close the lid after placing the pan in the bread machine.
Select the Bake cycle
Turn on the bread machine. Select the White/Basic setting, select the loaf size, and the crust color. Press start.
When the cycle is finished, carefully remove the pan from the bread maker and let it rest.
Remove the bread from the pan, put in a wire rack to Cool about 5 minutes. Slice

Nutrition Info: Calories: 146, Carbohydrates: 36g, Fat: 5.5g, Protein: 4g

Sunflower & Flax Seed Bread

Servings: 10

Cooking Time: 3 Hours

Ingredients:
Water – 1 1/3 cups.
Butter – 2 tbsps.
Honey – 3 tbsps.
Bread flour – 1 ½ cups.
Whole wheat flour – 1 1/3 cups.
Salt – 1 tsp.
Active dry yeast – 1 tsp.
Flax seeds – ½ cup.
Sunflower seeds – ½ cup.

Directions:
Add all ingredients except for sunflower seeds into the bread machine pan. Select basic setting then select light/medium crust and press start. Add sunflower seeds just before the final kneading cycle. Once loaf is done, remove the loaf pan from the machine. Allow it to cool for 10 minutes. Slice and serve.

Nutrition Info: Calories: 156, Carbohydrates: 40g, Fat: 5g, Protein: 4g

Honey-spice Egg Bread

Servings: 1 Loaf

Cooking Time: 10 Minutes

Ingredients:
12 slices bread (1½ pounds)
cup milk, at 80°F to 90°F
eggs, at room temperature
1½ tablespoons melted butter, cooled
2 tablespoons honey
1 teaspoon salt
1 teaspoon ground cinnamon
½ teaspoon ground cardamom
½ teaspoon ground nutmeg
3 cups white bread flour
2 teaspoons bread machine or instant yeast

Directions:
Preparing the Ingredients.
Choose the size of loaf of your preference and then measure the ingredients.
Add all of the ingredients mentioned previously in the list.
Close the lid after placing the pan in the bread machine.
Select the Bake cycle
Turn on the bread machine. Select the White/Basic setting, select the loaf size, and the crust color. Press start.
When the cycle is finished, carefully remove the pan from the bread maker and let it rest.
Remove the bread from the pan, put in a wire rack to Cool about 10 minutes. Slice

Nutrition Info: Calories: 143, Carbohydrates: 42g, Fat: 5.5g, Protein: 3g

Mix Seed Raisin Bread

Servings: 1 Loaf

Cooking Time: 10 Minutes

Ingredients:
16 slices bread (2 pounds)
1½ cups lukewarm milk
2 tablespoons unsalted butter, melted
2 tablespoons honey
1 teaspoon table salt
2½ cups white bread flour
¼ cup flaxseed
¼ cup sesame seeds
1½ cups whole-wheat flour
2¼ teaspoons bread machine yeast
½ cup raisins

Directions:
Preparing the Ingredients.
Choose the size of loaf of your preference and then measure the ingredients.
Add all of the ingredients mentioned previously in the list.
Close the lid after placing the pan in the bread machine.
Select the Bake cycle
Turn on the bread machine. Select the White/Basic setting, select the loaf size, and the crust color. Press start.
When the cycle is finished, carefully remove the pan from the bread maker and let it rest.
Remove the bread from the pan, put in a wire rack to Cool about 10 minutes. Slice

Nutrition Info: Calories: 132, Carbohydrates: 34g, Fat: 5g, Protein: 3g

Herb And Parmesan Bread

Servings: 10

Cooking Time: 3 Hours And 25 Minutes

Ingredients:
Lukewarm water – 1 1/3 cups
Oil – 2 tbsp.
Garlic – cloves, crushed
Fresh herbs – 3 tbsp., chopped (oregano, chives, basil, and rosemary)
Bread flour – 4 cups
Salt – 1 tsp.
Sugar – 1 tbsp.
Parmesan cheese – 4 tbsp., grated
Active dry yeast – 2 ¼ tsp.

Directions:
Add everything according to bread machine recommendations.
Select Basic cycle and Medium crust.
When done, remove the bread.
Cool, slice, and serve.

Nutrition Info: (Per Serving): Calories: 105, Total Fat: 5g,
Saturated Fat: 1g, Carbohydrates: 14g, Cholesterol: 2mg, Fiber: 2g,
Calcium: 94mg, Sodium: 412mg, Protein: 3g

Chia Seed Bread

Servings: 14 Slices

Cooking Time: 10 Minutes

Ingredients:
¼ cup chia seeds
¾ cup hot water
2⅜ cups water
¼ cup oil
½ lemon, zest and juice
1¾ cups white flour
1¾ cups whole wheat flour
2 tsp baking powder
1 tsp salt
1 Tbsp sugar
2½ tsp quick rise yeast

Directions:
Preparing the Ingredients
Add the chia seeds to a bowl, cover with hot water, mix well and let them stand until they are soaked and gelatinous, and don't feel warm to touch.
Add each ingredient to the bread machine in the order and at the temperature recommended by your bread machine manufacturer.
Select the Bake cycle
Close the lid, select the basic bread, medium crust setting on your bread machine, and press start.
When the mixing blade stops moving, open the machine and mix everything by hand with a spatula.
When the bread machine has finished baking, remove the bread and put it on a cooling rack.

Nutrition Info: Calories: 135, Carbohydrates: 29g, Fat: 3.5g, Protein: 3g

Orange Almond Bacon Bread

Servings: 10 Pcs

Cooking Time: 60 Minutes

Ingredients:
1 ½ cups almond flour
One tablespoon baking powder
7 oz bacon, diced   Two eggs
1 ½ cups cheddar cheese, shredded
Four tablespoons butter, melted
1/3 cup sour cream

Directions:
Add all ingredients to the bread machine.
Close the lid and choose the Sweet Bread mode.
After the cooking time is over, remove the machine's bread and rest for about 10 minutes.
Enjoy!

Nutrition Info: Calories: 307 Cal, Fat: 26g, Carbohydrate: 3g, Protein: 14g

Chocolate Mint Bread

Servings: 1 Loaf

Cooking Time: 10 Minutes

Ingredients:
12 slices bread (1½ pounds)
1 cup milk, at 80°F to 90°F
⅛ teaspoon mint extract
1½ tablespoons butter, melted and cooled
¼ cup sugar
1 teaspoon salt
1½ tablespoons unsweetened cocoa powder
3 cups white bread flour
1¾ teaspoons bread machine or instant yeast
½ cup semisweet chocolate chips

Directions:
Preparing the Ingredients.
Choose the size of loaf of your preference and then measure the ingredients.
Add all of the ingredients mentioned previously in the list.
Close the lid after placing the pan in the bread machine.
Select the Bake cycle
Turn on the bread machine. Select the White/Basic setting, select the loaf size, and the crust color. Press start.
When the cycle is finished, carefully remove the pan from the bread maker and let it rest.
Remove the bread from the pan, put in a wire rack to Cool about 5 minutes. Slice

Nutrition Info: Calories: 136, Carbohydrates: 46g, Fat: 5g, Protein: 4g

Italian Pine Nut Bread

Servings: 10

Cooking Time: 3 Hours 30 Minutes

Ingredients:
Water – 1 cup+ 2 tbsps.
Bread flour – 3 cups.
Sugar – 2 tbsps.
Salt – 1 tsp.
Active dry yeast – 1 ¼ tsps.
Basil pesto – 1/3 cup.
Flour – 2 tbsps.
Pine nuts – 1/3 cup.

Directions:
In a small bowl, mix basil pesto and flour until well blended. Add pine nuts and stir well. Add water, bread flour, sugar, salt, and yeast into the bread machine pan. Select basic setting then select medium crust and press start. Add basil pesto mixture just before the final kneading cycle. Once loaf is done, remove the loaf pan from the machine. Allow it to cool for 10 minutes. Slice and serve.

Nutrition Info: Calories: 126, Carbohydrates: 28g, Fat: 4g, Protein: 6g

Anise Lemon Bread

Servings: 1 Loaf

Cooking Time: 10 Minutes

Ingredients:
12 slice bread (1½ pounds)
¾ cup water, at 80°F to 90°F
1 egg, at room temperature
¼ cup butter, melted and cooled
¼ cup honey
½ teaspoon salt
1 teaspoon anise seed
1 teaspoon lemon zest
3 cups white bread flour
2 teaspoons bread machine or instant yeast

Directions:
Preparing the Ingredients.
Choose the size of loaf of your preference and then measure the ingredients.
Add all of the ingredients mentioned previously in the list.
Close the lid after placing the pan in the bread machine.
Select the Bake cycle
Turn on the bread machine. Select the White/Basic setting, select the loaf size, and the crust color. Press start.
When the cycle is finished, carefully remove the pan from the bread maker and let it rest.
Remove the bread from the pan, put in a wire rack to Cool about 10 minutes. Slice

Nutrition Info: Calories: 149, Carbohydrates: 23g, Fat: 3.5g, Protein: 5g

Egg And Seed Buns

Servings: 8 Pcs

Cooking Time: 50 Minutes

Ingredients:
Two egg whites
1 cup sunflower seeds, ground
¼ cup flax seeds, ground
5 Tbsp. psyllium husks
cup boiling water
tsp. baking powder
Salt to taste

Directions:
Combine all the dry ingredients.
Add the egg whites and blend until smooth.
Add boiling water and keep whisking.
Line a baking sheet with parchment paper and drop the dough on it one spoonful at a time to form buns.
Bake at 356F for 50 minutes.
Serve.

Nutrition Info: Calories: 91 Cal, Fat: 4.2g, Carb: 12.1g, Protein: 3.3g

Olive Bread

Servings: 14 Slices

Cooking Time: 3 H.

Ingredients:
½ cup brine from olive jar
Add warm water (110°F) To make 1½ cup when combined with brine
Tbsp olive oil
cups bread flour
1⅔ cups whole wheat flour
1½ tsp salt
2 Tbsp sugar
1½ tsp dried leaf basil
2 tsp active dry yeast
⅔ cup finely chopped Kalamata olives

Directions:
Add each ingredient except the olives to the bread machine in the order and at the temperature recommended by your bread machine manufacturer.
Close the lid, select the wheat, medium crust setting on your bread machine and press start.
Add the olives 10 minutes before the last kneading cycle ends.
When the bread machine has finished baking, remove the bread and put it on a cooling rack.

Nutrition Info: Calories: 116 Cal, Fat: 4.6g, Carb: 14.1g, Protein: 3.6g

Cinnamon Bread

Servings: 1 Loaf

Cooking Time: 10 Minutes

Ingredients:
12 slices bread (1½ pounds)
1 cup milk, at 80°F to 90°F
1 egg, at room temperature
¼ cup melted butter, cooled
½ cup sugar
½ teaspoon salt
1½ teaspoons ground cinnamon
3 cups white bread flour
2 teaspoons bread machine or active dry yeast

Directions:
Preparing the Ingredients.
Choose the size of loaf of your preference and then measure the ingredients.
Add all of the ingredients mentioned previously in the list.
Close the lid after placing the pan in the bread machine.
Select the Bake cycle
Turn on the bread machine. Select the White/Basic setting, select the loaf size, and the crust color. Press start.
When the cycle is finished, carefully remove the pan from the bread maker and let it rest.
Remove the bread from the pan, put in a wire rack to Cool about 10 minutes. Slice

Nutrition Info: Calories: 101 Cal, Fat: 4.8g, Carb: 15g, Protein: 6.3g

Oatmeal Seed Bread

Servings: 1 Loaf

Cooking Time: 10 Minutes

Ingredients:
12 slice bread (1½ pounds)
1⅛ cups water, at 80°F to 90°F
3 tablespoons melted butter, cooled
3 tablespoons light brown sugar
1½ teaspoons salt
3 tablespoons raw sunflower seeds
3 tablespoons pumpkin seeds
2 tablespoons sesame seeds
1 teaspoon anise seeds
1 cup quick oats
2¼ cups white bread flour
1½ teaspoons bread machine or instant yeast

Directions:
Preparing the Ingredients.
Choose the size of loaf of your preference and then measure the ingredients.
Add all of the ingredients mentioned previously in the list.
Close the lid after placing the pan in the bread machine.
Select the Bake cycle
Turn on the bread machine. Select the White/Basic setting, select the loaf size, and the crust color. Press start.
When the cycle is finished, carefully remove the pan from the bread maker and let it rest.
Remove the bread from the pan, put in a wire rack to Cool about 5 minutes. Slice

Nutrition Info: Calories: 123 Cal, Fat: 6.2g, Carb: 14, Protein: 7g

Whole-wheat Seed Bread

Servings: 1 Loaf

Cooking Time: 10 Minutes

Ingredients:
12 slice bread (1½ pounds)
1⅛ cups water, at 80°F to 90°F
1½ tablespoons honey
1½ tablespoons melted butter, cooled
¾ teaspoon salt
2½ cups whole-wheat flour
¾ cup white bread flour
3 tablespoons raw sunflower seeds
1 tablespoon sesame seeds
1½ teaspoons bread machine or instant yeast

Directions:
Preparing the Ingredients.
Choose the size of loaf of your preference and then measure the ingredients.
Add all of the ingredients mentioned previously in the list.
Close the lid after placing the pan in the bread machine.
Select the Bake cycle
Turn on the bread machine. Select the Whole-Wheat/Whole-Grain bread, select the loaf size, and select light or medium crust. Press start.
When the cycle is finished, carefully remove the pan from the bread maker and let it rest.
Remove the bread from the pan, put in a wire rack to Cool about 5 minutes. Slice

Nutrition Info: Calories: 125 Cal, Fat: 5.5g, Carb: 15g, Protein: 6.5g

Garlic Herb Bread

Servings: 8

Cooking Time: 3 Hours And 25 Minutes

Ingredients:
1% milk – 1 cup, warm
Light butter - 1 tbsp.
White sugar – 1 tbsp.
Salt – 1 ½ tsp.
Italian seasoning – 1 ½ tsp.
Garlic powder – 3 tsp.
White flour – 3 cups
Active dry yeast – 2 tsp.

Directions:
Add everything according to bread machine recommendations.
Select Basic bread cycle and press Start.
Remove the bread when done.
Cool, slice, and serve.

Nutrition Info: (Per Serving): Calories: 213, Total Fat: 2.8g,
Saturated Fat: 1.4g, Carbohydrates: 40g, Cholesterol: 7mg, Fiber: 1.6g,
Calcium: 46mg, Sodium: 465mg, Protein: 6.4g

Pesto Nut Bread

Servings: 14 Slices

Cooking Time: 10 Minutes

Ingredients:
1 cup plus 2 Tbsp water
3 cups Gold Medal Better for Bread flour
2 Tbsp sugar
tsp salt
1¼ tsp bread machine or quick active dry yeast
For the pesto filling:
⅓ cup basil pesto
Tbsp Gold Medal Better for Bread flour
⅓ cup pine nuts

Directions:
Preparing the Ingredients
Add each ingredient to the bread machine in the order and at the temperature recommended by your bread machine manufacturer.
Select the Bake cycle
Close the lid, select the basic bread, medium crust setting on your bread machine, and press start.
In a small bowl, combine pesto and 2 Tbsp of flour until well blended. Stir in the pine nuts. Add the filling 5 minutes before the last kneading cycle ends.
When the bread machine has finished baking, remove the bread and put it on a cooling rack.

Nutrition Info: Calories: 132, Carbohydrates: 4g, Protein: 7g, Fat: 15g

Sesame French Bread

Servings: 14 Slices

Cooking Time: 3 H. 15 Min.

Ingredients:
⅞ cup water
1 Tbsp butter, softened
3 cups bread flour
2 tsp sugar
tsp salt
tsp yeast
2 Tbsp sesame seeds toasted

Directions:
Add each ingredient to the bread machine in the order and at the temperature recommended by your bread machine manufacturer. Close the lid, select the French bread, medium crust setting on your bread machine and press start.
When the bread machine has finished baking, remove the bread and put it on a cooling rack.

Nutrition Info: Calories: 124, Carbohydrates: 6.3g, Protein: 5.8g, Fat: 13.5g

Coffee Raisin Bread

Servings: 10

Cooking Time: 3 Hours

Ingredients:
Active dry yeast – 2 ½ tsps.
Ground cloves – ¼ tsp.
Ground allspice – ¼ tsp.
Ground cinnamon – 1 tsp.
Sugar – 3 tbsps.
Egg – 1, lightly beaten
Olive oil – 3 tbsps.
Strong brewed coffee – 1 cup.
Bread flour – 3 cups.
Raisins – ¾ cup.
Salt – 1 ½ tsps.

Directions:
Add all ingredients except for raisins into the bread machine pan. Select basic setting then select light/medium crust and press start. Add raisins just before the final kneading cycle. Once loaf is done, remove the loaf pan from the machine. Allow it to cool for 10 minutes. Slice and serve.

Nutrition Info: Calories: 118, Carbohydrates: 4.7g, Protein: 7g, Fat: 15g

Semolina Bread

Servings: 6 Pcs

Cooking Time: One Hour

Ingredients:
Almond fine flour, one cup
Semolina flour, one cup
Yeast, one teaspoon
An egg
Salt, one teaspoon
Stevia powder, two teaspoons
Olive oil extra virgin, two teaspoons
Water warm, one cup
Sesame seeds, two teaspoons

Directions:
Get a mixing container and combine the almond flour, semolina flour, salt, and stevia powder.
In another mixing container, combine the egg
extra virgin olive oil, and warm water.
By instructions on your machine's manual, pour the ingredients in the bread pan and follow how to mix in the yeast.
Put the bread pan in the machine, select the basic bread setting together with the bread size and crust type, if available, then press start once you have closed the machine's lid.
When the bread is ready, open the lid and spread the sesame seeds at the top and close for a few minutes.
By using oven mitts, remove the pan from the machine. Use a stainless spatula to extract the pan's bread and turn the pan upside down on a metallic rack where the bread will cool off before slicing it.

Nutrition Info: Calories: 100, Carbohydrates: 2.8g, Protein: 5g, Fat: 14g

Gingered Spice Bread

Servings: 16

Cooking Time: 3 Hours And 25 Minutes

Ingredients:
Milk – ¾ cup
Molasses – 3 tbsp.
Egg – 1
Butter – 2 tbsp.
Salt – ¾ tsp.
Bread flour – 3 cups
Ground ginger – 1 tsp.
Ground cinnamon – ½ tsp.
Ground cloves – ¼ tsp.
Bread machine yeast – 2 tsp.

Directions:
Add everything to the bread pan in the order suggested by the manufacturer.
Select Basic/White bread cycle, choose Light or Medium crust. Press Start.
Remove the bread when done.
Cool, slice, and serve.

Nutrition Info: (Per Serving): Calories: 123, Total Fat: 2.4g, Saturated Fat: 1.3g, Carbohydrates: 21.6g, Cholesterol: 18.6mg, Fiber: 0.8g, Calcium: 22mg, Sodium: 131.4mg, Protein: 3.4g

Nutty Wheat Bread

Servings: 1 Loaf

Cooking Time: 10 Minutes

Ingredients:
12 slice bread (1½ pounds)
1½ cups water, at 80°F to 90°F
2 tablespoons melted butter, cooled
tablespoon sugar
1½ teaspoons salt
1¼ cups whole-wheat flour
cups white bread flour
1¼ teaspoons bread machine or instant yeast
2 tablespoons chopped almonds
2 tablespoons chopped pecans
2 tablespoons sunflower seeds

Directions:
Preparing the Ingredients.
Place the ingredients, except the almonds, pecans, and seeds, in your bread machine as recommended by the manufacturer.
Select the Bake cycle
Turn on the bread machine. Select the White/Basic setting, select the loaf size, and the crust color. Press start.
When the cycle is finished, carefully remove the pan from the bread maker and let it rest.
Remove the bread from the pan, put in a wire rack to Cool about 5 minutes. Slice

Nutrition Info: Calories: 123, Carbohydrates: 6g, Protein: 7g, Fat: 13g

Savoury Herb Blend Bread

Servings: 16 Pcs

Cooking Time: One Hour

Ingredients:
1 cup almond flour
1/2 cup coconut flour
1 cup parmesan cheese
3/4 tsp baking powder
Three eggs
3 tbsp coconut oil
1/2 tbsp rosemary
1/2 tsp thyme, ground
1/2 tsp sage, ground
1/2 tsp oregano
1/2 tsp garlic powder
1/2 tsp onion powder
1/4 tsp salt

Directions:
Light beat eggs and coconut oil together before adding to the bread machine pan.
Add all the remaining ingredients to the bread machine pan.
Set the bread machine to the gluten-free setting. 4.   When the bread is finished, remove the bread
machine pan from the bread machine.
Let cool slightly before transferring to a cooling rack.
You can store your bread for up to 7 days.

Nutrition Info: Calories: 170, Carbohydrates: 6g, Protein: 9g, Fat: 15g

Pumpkin Coconut Almond Bread

Servings: 12 Slices

Cooking Time: 5 Minutes

Ingredients:
1/3 cup vegetable oil
3 large eggs
1 1/2 cups canned pumpkin puree
1 cup sugar
1 1/2 teaspoons baking powder
1/2 teaspoon baking soda
1/4 teaspoon salt
1 tablespoon allspice
3 cups all-purpose flour
1/2 cup coconut flakes, plus a small handful for the topping
2/3 cup slivered almonds, plus a tablespoonful for the topping
Non-stick cooking spray

Directions:
Preparing the Ingredients
Spray bread maker pan with non-stick cooking spray. Mix oil, eggs, and pumpkin in a large mixing bowl.
Mix remaining ingredients together in a separate mixing bowl. Add wet ingredients to bread maker pan, and dry ingredients on top.
Select the Bake cycle
Select Dough cycle and press Start. Open lid and sprinkle top of bread with reserved coconut and almonds.
Set to Rapid for 1 hour 30 minutes and bake. Cool for 10 minutes on a wire rack before serving.

Nutrition Info: Calories: 161, Carbohydrates: 5.5g, Protein: 6.2g, Fat: 17g

AD FROM AROUND THE WORLD

"po Boy" Rolls From New Orleans

Servings: 6 Rolls

Cooking Time: 25 Minutes

Ingredients:
1 cup water
1 tbsp granulated sugar
1 ½ tsp salt
1 tbsp extra-virgin olive oil
3 cups plain bread flour
1 tbsp instant dry yeast

Directions:
Add the ingredients into the bread machine as per the order of the ingredients listed above or follow your bread machine's instruction manual.

Select the dough setting.

When the dough is ready, place it onto a floured surface and split it into six even pieces. Then transfer them onto a parchment-lined baking tray.

Switch on the oven for 2 minutes, then turn it off. Place the dough into the oven and allow it to rise for one hour and 30 minutes or until it has doubled in size then remove.

Preheat your oven to 400 °F and then place an oven-proof dish on the lowest rack.

Using a sharp knife make slashes into the dough and mist with water.

When the oven has reached 400°F, place the dough into the oven and bake for 20 minutes or until the rolls, have reached a golden color.

When ready, turn the bread out onto a drying rack and allow it to cool, then serve.

Nutrition Info: (Per Serving): Calories: 280 kcal, Total fat: 3.5g, Saturated fat: 0g, Cholesterol: 0g, Total carbohydrates: 52g, Dietary fiber: 2g, Sodium: 600mg, Protein: 8g

Healthy Low Carb Bread

Servings: 8 Slices

Cooking Time: 35 Minutes

Ingredients:
2/3 cup coconut flour
2/3 cup coconut oil (softened not melted)
Nine eggs
2 tsp. Cream of tartar
¾ tsp. xanthan gum
1 tsp. Baking soda
¼ tsp. salt

Directions:
Preheat the oven to 350F.
Grease a loaf pan with 1 to 2 tsp. Melted coconut oil and place it in the freezer to harden.
Add eggs into a bowl and mix for 2 minutes with a hand mixer.
Add coconut oil into the eggs and mix.
Add dry ingredients to a second bowl and whisk until mixed.
Put the dry ingredients into the egg mixture and mix on low speed with a hand mixer until dough is formed and the mixture is incorporated.
Add the dough into the prepared loaf pan, transfer into the preheated oven, and bake for 35 minutes.
Take out the bread pan from the oven.
Cool, slice, and serve.

Nutrition Info: Calories: 229, Fat: 25.5g, Carb: 6.5g, Protein: 8.5g

Russian Rye Bread

Servings: 12

Cooking Time: 3 Hours

Ingredients:
1 1/4 cups warm water
1 3/4 cups rye flour
3/4 cups whole wheat flour
tablespoons malt (or beer kit mixture)
tablespoon molasses
tablespoons white vinegar
teaspoon salt
1/2 tablespoon coriander seeds
1/2 tablespoon caraway seeds
teaspoons active dry yeast

Directions:
Mix dry ingredients together in a bowl, except for yeast.
Add wet ingredients to bread pan first; top with dry ingredients.
Make a well in the center of the dry ingredients and add the yeast.
Press Basic bread cycle, choose medium crust color, and press Start.
Remove from bread pan and allow to cool on a wire rack before
serving.

Nutrition Info: Calories: 141, Sodium: 196mg, Dietary Fiber: 5.1g,
Fat: 0.8g, Carbs: 29.7g, Protein: 5g

Sauerkraut Bread

Servings: 1 Loaf (22 Slices)

Cooking Time: 1 Hour And 30 Minutes

Ingredients:
cup lukewarm water (80 degrees F)
¼ cup cabbage brine
½ cup finely chopped cabbage
Two tablespoons sunflower oil
Two teaspoons white sugar
1½ teaspoons salt
1/3 cups rye flour
2 1/3 cups wheat flour
Two teaspoons dry kvass
Two teaspoons active dry yeast

Directions:
Prepare all of the ingredients for your bread and measuring means (a cup, a spoon, kitchen scales).
Finely chop the sauerkraut.
Carefully measure the ingredients into the pan.
Place all of the ingredients into a bucket in the right order, follow your manual bread machine.
Close the cover.
Select the program of your bread machine to BASIC and choose the crust colour to
DARK. Press START.
Wait until the program completes.
When done, take the bucket out and let it cool for 5-10 minutes.
Shake the loaf from the pan and let cool for 30 minutes on a cooling rack.
Slice, serve and enjoy the taste of fragrant homemade bread.

Nutrition Info: Calories 297, Total Fat 4.9g, Saturated Fat 0.5g, Cholesterol 0g, Sodium 442mg, Total Carbohydrate 55.5g, Dietary Fiber 9.7g, Total Sugars 1.6g, Protein 9.5g

Corn Poppy Seeds Sour Cream Bread

Servings: 1 Loaf (16 Slices)

Cooking Time: 1 Hour And 30 Minutes

Ingredients:
3½ cups all-purpose flour
1¾ cups of cornflour
5 ounces sour cream
Two tablespoons corn oil
Two teaspoons active dry yeast
Two teaspoons salt
16 ¼ ounces lukewarm water
poppy seeds for sprinkling

Directions:
Select the program of your bread machine to BASIC and choose the crust colour to
MEDIUM.
Press START.
After the kneading brush the loaf with the water and sprinkle with poppy seeds.
Wait until the program completes.
When done, take the bucket out and let it cool for 5-10 minutes.
Shake the loaf from the pan and let cool for 30 minutes on a cooling rack.
Slice, serve and enjoy the taste of fragrant homemade bread.

Nutrition Info: Calories 223, Total Fat 4.8g, Saturated Fat 1.6g, Cholesterol 4g, Sodium 297mg, Total Carbohydrate 39.9g, Total Sugars 0.2g, Protein 5.2g

French Ham Bread

Servings: 10

Cooking Time: 3 Hours And 27 Minutes

Ingredients:
Wheat bread flour – 3 1/3 cups
Ham – 1 cup, chopped
Milk powder – ½ cup
Sugar – 1 ½ tbsp.
Fresh yeast – 1 tsp.
Kosher salt – 1 tsp.
Parmesan cheese – 2 tbsp., grated
Lukewarm water – 1 1/3 cups
Oil – 2 tbsp.

Directions:
Add everything (except for the ham) in the bread machine according to
bread machine recommendations.
Select French bread and Medium crust.
Add ham after the beep.
Remove the bread when done.
Cool, slice, and serve.

Nutrition Info: (Per Serving): Calories: 287, Total Fat: 5.5g,
Saturated Fat: 1.1g, Carbohydrates: 47.2g, Cholesterol: 11mg,
Fiber: 1.7g, Calcium: 65mg, Sodium: 557mg, Protein: 11.4g

Mexican Sweetbread

Servings: 12

Cooking Time: 3 Hours And 25 Minutes

Ingredients:
Milk – 1 cup
Butter – ¼ cup
Egg – 1
Sugar – ¼ cup
Salt – 1 tsp.
Bread flour – 3 cups
Yeast – 1 ½ tsp.

Directions:
Place all ingredients in the bread machine according to bread machine recommendations.
Select Basic or Sweet cycle. Press Start.
Remove the bread when done.
Cool, slice, and serve.

Nutrition Info: (Per Serving): Calories: 184.3, Total Fat: 5.3g, Saturated Fat: 1.3g, Carbohydrates: 29.2g, Cholesterol: 20.5mg, Fiber: 0.9g, Calcium: 38mg, Sodium: 254.8mg, Protein: 4.7g

Mediterranean Bread

Servings: 8

Cooking Time: 3 Hours And 25 Minutes

Ingredients:
Water – 1 cup
Crumbled feta cheese – 1/3 cup
Garlic cloves – 3, minced
Salt – 1 ¼ tsp.
Honey – 1 tsp.
Olive oil – 1 tbsp.
Bread flour – 3 ¼ cups
Kalamata olive – ½ cup, sliced
Dried oregano – 2 tsp.
Bread machine yeast – ¾ tsp.

Directions:
Add everything in the bread machine according to bread machine recommendations.
Select Basic cycle and press Start.
Remove the bread when done.
Cool, slice, and serve.

Nutrition Info: (Per Serving): Calories: 237, Total Fat: 4.5g, Saturated Fat: 1.4g, Carbohydrates: 42.4g, Cholesterol: 5.6mg, Fiber: 1.9g, Calcium: 22mg, Sodium: 497.3mg, Protein: 6.5g

Matcha Coconut Cookies

Servings: 12 Pcs

Cooking Time: 12 Minutes

Ingredients:
1/3 cup Almond Flour
1/3 cup Coconut Flour
2 tbsp Matcha Powder
½ cup Swerve Granular Sweetener
½ tsp Baking Powder
½ cup Coconut Oil
1 Whole Egg

Directions:
Put Whisk together almond flour, coconut flour, sweetener, matcha, and baking powder in a bowl.
Add in the egg and coconut oil. Mix until well combined.
Scoop the dough into a baking sheet lined with parchment. Press slightly to flatten.
Bake for 12 minutes.

Nutrition Info: Kcal per serve: 112, Fat: 12g, Protein: 2g, Carbs: 1g

Pita Bread

Servings: 8 Pcs

Cooking Time: 20 Minutes

Ingredients:
3 cups of all-purpose flour
1 1/8 cups warm water
One tablespoon of vegetable oil
One teaspoon salt
1 ½ teaspoon active dry yeast
One active teaspoon white sugar

Directions:
Place all the ingredients in your bread pan.
Select the dough setting. Hit the start button.
The machine beeps after the dough rises adequately.
Turn the dough on a floured surface.
Roll and stretch the dough gently into a 12-inch rope.
Cut into eight pieces with a knife.
Now roll each piece into a ball. It should be smooth.
Roll each ball into a 7-inch circle. Keep covered with a towel on a floured top for 30 minutes for the pita to rise. It should get puffy slightly.
Preheat your oven to 260 degrees C.
Keep the pitas on your wire cake rack. Transfer to the oven rack directly.
Bake the pitas for 5 minutes. They should be puffed. The top should start to brown.
Take out from the oven. Keep the pitas immediately in a sealed paper bag. You can also cover using a damp kitchen towel.
Split the top edge or cut into half once the pitas are soft. You can also have the whole pitas if you want.

Nutrition Info: Calories 191, Carbohydrates: 37g, Total Fat 3g, Cholesterol 0mg, Protein 5g, Fiber 1g, Sugar 1g, Sodium 293mg, Potassium 66mg

Sweet Dinner Rolls

Servings: 1 Loaf

Cooking Time: 30 Minutes

Ingredients:
2 ½ cups almond flour
1 cup coconut flour
½ cup butter
¼ cup no-calorie sweetener of your choice
¾ teaspoons salt
Two eggs
1 cup milk

Directions:
Add the wet ingredients into the bread pan, and then the dry ingredients.
Use the "Manual" or "Dough" mode of the bread machine.
Once done, put the dough in a lightly oiled bowl.
Preheat the oven to 375F.
Divide and shape the dough into 16 pieces.
Cover and just let the dough rise for 30 minutes.
Bake until golden brown.
Cooldown and serve.

Nutrition Info: Calories: 125, Carbohydrates: 4g, Fat: 9g, Protein: 8g

Pizza Dough Recipe

Servings: 6 Servings

Cooking Time: 1 Hour And 30 Minutes

Ingredients:
2 cups plain bread flour
1 tbsp unsalted butter, softened
1 tbsp sugar
1 tsp instant dry yeast
1 tsp salt
½ cup lukewarm water

Directions:
Add the ingredients into the bread machine as per the order of the ingredients listed above or follow your bread machine's instruction manual.

Select the dough setting and press start.

Ten minutes into the bread machine's cycle, check on the dough to ensure that the ingredients have mixed evenly and that the dough is not too wet or dry.

Preheat your oven to 400 °F.

When ready, turn the dough out onto a floured surface and knead into a pizza or pan dish shape.

Top with your desired toppings and bake for 20 to 25 minutes.

Nutrition Info: (Per Serving): Calories: 536 kcal, Total fat: 7g, Saturated fat: 4g, Cholesterol: 15mg, Total carbohydrates: 102g, Dietary fiber: 4g, Sodium: 1221mg, Protein: 14 g

Garlic And Herb Bread

Servings: 1 Pound Loaf

Cooking Time: 2 Hours

Ingredients:
Unsalted butter, diced :1 tbsp
Lukewarm 1% milk :1 cup
White all-purpose flour :3 cups
Italian seasoning :1 ½ tsp
Garlic powder :3 tsp
Sugar :1 tbsp
Salt :1 ½ tsp
Instant dry yeast :2 tsp

Directions:
Add the ingredients into the bread machine as per the order of the ingredients listed above or follow your bread machine's instruction manual.
Select the basic setting and medium crust function.
When ready, turn the bread out onto a drying rack and allow it to cool, then serve.

Nutrition Info: (Per Serving): Calories: 203.8 kcal, Total fat: 2.2g, Saturated fat: 1.2g, Cholesterol: 5.4mg, Total carbohydrates: 39g, Dietary fiber: 1.5g, Sodium: 451.4mg, Protein: 6.2g

Sweet Challa

Servings: 1 Loaf

Cooking Time: 45 Minutes

Ingredients:
1 ½ cup cream cheese
cup protein powder, unflavored and unsweetened
2/3 cup protein powder, vanilla flavour and unsweetened
1/3 cup no-calorie sweetener of your choice
¼ cup dried cranberries
¼ cup butter
¼ cup almond flour
½ teaspoons baking powder
One teaspoon xanthan gum
½ teaspoon salt
1/3 teaspoon salt
Four eggs, beaten
¼ cup heavy cream
¼ cup oil

Directions:
Set aside two tablespoons of the beaten eggs for later use.
Put the wet ingredients first, then the dry ingredients into the bread pan.
Press the "Manual" or "Dough" setting on the bread machine.
Once completed, transfer the dough to a surface that has been lightly dusted with almond flour.
Remove the air bubbles by punching the dough.
Divide the dough into 3.
Roll each piece until it becomes 16 inches long.
Braid the three pieces together on a lightly greased baking sheet.
Allow the dough to rise for about 30 minutes while preheating the oven to 400F.
Brush the dough on the top with the reserved eggs from earlier.
Bake for 45 minutes, or until it is golden brown.

Nutrition Info: Calories: 158, Carbohydrates: 2g, Fat: 13g, Protein: 9g

Challah

Servings: 12

Cooking Time: 1 Hour 40 Minutes

Ingredients:
1/2 cup warm water
1 package active dry yeast
1 tablespoon sugar
3 tablespoons butter, softened
1/2 teaspoon kosher salt
2 to 2 1/2 cups kosher all-purpose flour
2 eggs
1 egg yolk
1 teaspoon water

Directions:
Add sugar and salt to bread maker pan.
Add butter, eggs, then water.
Add flour and yeast.
Select Dough cycle and press Start.
Transfer dough to a large mixing bowl sprayed with non-stick cooking spray. Spray
dough with non-stick cooking spray and cover. Let rise in a warm place until doubled in size; about 45 minutes.
Punch dough down. Remove dough to lightly floured surface; pat dough and shape into a 10-by-6-inch rectangle.
Divide into 3 equal strips with a pizza cutter. Braid strips and place into a 9-by-5-inch loaf pan sprayed with non-stick cooking spray. Cover and let rise in warm place for about 30 to 45 minutes.
Beat egg yolk with 1 teaspoon water and baste loaf.
Bake at 375°F for 25 to 30 minutes, or until golden.
Let cool on a rack for 5 minutes before removing from loaf pan and serve.

Nutrition Info: Calories: 64, Sodium: 129mg, Dietary Fiber: 0.3g, Fat: 4g, Carbs: 5.2g, Protein: 1.9g.

Zesty Poppy Seed Bread

Servings: 1 Loaf

Cooking Time: 1 Hour And 30 Minutes

Ingredients:
9.5 ounces almond flour
Two lemons, zest only
½ cup no-calorie sweetener of your choice
Three tablespoons butter
Two tablespoons poppy seeds
½ teaspoon baking powder
Six eggs
Two tablespoons lemon juice
Two tablespoons water

Directions:
Put the wet ingredients, followed by the dry ingredients, into the bread pan.
Select the "Quick" or "Cake" mode of your bread machine.
Allow the cycles to be completed.
Remove the bread pan from the machine but keep the bread in the container for another 10 minutes.
Take out the bread from the bread pan, and let it cool down completely before slicing.

Nutrition Info: Calories: 70, Carbohydrates: 6g, Fat: 17g, Protein: 9g

No-bake Butter Cookies

Servings: 8 Pcs

Cooking Time: 0 Minutes

Ingredients:
½ cup almond flour
1½ tbsp butter
1 tbsp Swerve
½ tsp vanilla extract
1 pinch salt

Directions:
Mix all the ingredients in a bowl to prepare the cookie batter.
Spoon out the batter onto a cookie sheet positioned on a baking tray.
Put the tray in the refrigerator and refrigerate for about 1 hour 10 minutes.
Serve the cookies.

Nutrition Info: Calories: 125 Cal, Fat: 3.2g, Cholesterol: 11mg, Sodium: 75mg, Carbohydrates: 3,6 g

Raisin Bread

Servings: 1 Pound Loaf

Cooking Time: 3 Hours

Ingredients:
Lukewarm water :⅙ cup
Unsalted butter, diced :1 ¼ tbsp
Plain bread flour :2 cups
Orange zest :1 pinch
Ground cinnamon :1 ⅓ tsp
Ground clove :1 pinch
Ground nutmeg :1 pinch
Salt :1 pinch
Sugar :1 ¼ tbsp
Active dry yeast :1 ½ tsp
Raisins :½ cup

Directions:
Add the ingredients into the bread machine as per the order of the ingredients listed above or follow your bread machine's instruction manual. Do not add the raisins in yet.
Select the nut or raisin setting and medium crust function.
When the machine signals you to add the raisins, do so.
When ready, turn the bread out onto a drying rack and allow it to cool, then serve.

Nutrition Info: (Per Serving): Calories: 78 kcal, Total fat: 1g, Saturated fat: 1g, Cholesterol: 3mg, Total carbohydrates: 16g, Dietary fiber: 1g, Sodium: 106mg, Protein: 2g

Country-styled White Bread

Servings: 1 Pound Loaf

Cooking Time: 2 Hours And 5 Minutes

Ingredients:
Lukewarm water :1 ½ cups
Extra-virgin olive oil :1 ½ tbsp
Plain bread flour :1 cup
White all-purpose Flour :2 ½ cups
Baking soda :¼ tsp
Sugar :1 ½ tsp
Salt :1 pinch
Bread machine yeast :2 ½ tsp

Directions:
Add the ingredients into the bread machine as per the order of the ingredients listed above or follow your bread machine's instruction manual.
Select the rapid setting and the medium crust function.
When ready, turn the bread out onto a drying rack and allow it to cool, then serve.

Nutrition Info: (Per Serving): Calories: 122 kcal, Total fat: 5g, Saturated fat: 1g, Cholesterol: 0mg, Total carbohydrates: 17g, Dietary fiber: 2g, Sodium: 394mg, Protein: 2g

Italian Herb Pizza Dough

Servings: 1 Crust

Cooking Time: 1 Hour And 30 Minutes

Ingredients:
Warm water – 1 cup
Olive oil – 3 tbsp.
White sugar – 3 tbsp.
Sea salt – 1 tsp.
All-purpose flour – 3 cups
Minced garlic – 1 tsp.
Dried oregano – ¼ tsp.
Dried basil – ¼ tsp.
Ground black pepper – ¼ tsp.
Dried cilantro – ¼ tsp.
Paprika – ¼ tsp.
Active dry yeast – 2 ¼ tsp.

Directions:
Add everything in the bread machine according to bread machine recommendations.
Select the Dough cycle and press Start.
Remove when done.
Allow the dough to rise 30 minutes before using.

Nutrition Info: (Per Serving): Calories: 476, Total Fat: 11.2g, Saturated Fat: 1.6g, Carbohydrates: 82.3g, Cholesterol: 0mg, Fiber: 3.2g, Calcium: 23.5mg, Sodium: 445.3mg, Protein: 10.7g

Rice Bread

Servings: 1 Loaf (16 Slices)

Cooking Time: 1 Hour And 30 Minutes

Ingredients:
4½ cups all-purpose flour
1 cup of rice, cooked
One whole egg beaten
Two tablespoons of milk powder
Two teaspoons active dry yeast
Two tablespoons butter, melted
One tablespoon sugar
Two teaspoon salt
1¼ cups lukewarm water (80 degrees F)

Directions:
Prepare all of the ingredients for your bread and measuring means (a cup, a spoon, kitchen scales).
Carefully measure the ingredients into the pan.
Place all of the ingredients into a bread bucket in the right order, follow your manual bread machine.
Close the cover.
Select the program of your bread machine to BASIC and choose the crust colour to
MEDIUM.
Press START.
Wait until the program completes.
When done, take the bucket out and let it cool for 5-10 minutes.
Shake the loaf from the pan and let cool for 30 minutes on a cooling rack.
Slice, serve and enjoy the taste of fragrant homemade bread.

Nutrition Info: Calories 197, Total Fat 2.1g, Saturated Fat 1.1g, Cholesterol 14g, Sodium 311mg, Total Carbohydrate 37.8g, Dietary Fiber 1.3g, Total Sugars 1.4g, Protein 5.6g

Walnut Bread

Servings: 1 Loaf (20 Slices)

Cooking Time: 2 Hours

Ingredients:
4 cups (500 g) wheat flour, sifted
½ cup (130 ml) lukewarm water (80 degrees F)
½ cup (120 ml) lukewarm milk (80 degrees F)
Two whole eggs
½ cup walnuts, fried and chopped
One tablespoon walnut oil
One tablespoon brown sugar
One teaspoon salt
One teaspoon active dry yeast

Directions:
Prepare all of the ingredients for your bread and measuring means (a cup, a spoon, kitchen scales).
Carefully measure the ingredients into the pan.
Place all of the ingredients into the bread bucket in the right order.
Follow your manual bread machine.
Close the cover.
Select your bread machine's program to FRENCH BREAD and choose the crust colour to MEDIUM. 6. Press START.
Wait until the program completes.
When done, take the bucket out and let it cool for 5-10 minutes.
Shake the loaf from the pan and let cool for 30 minutes on a cooling rack.
Slice, serve and enjoy the taste of fragrant homemade bread.

Nutrition Info: Calories 257, Total Fat 6.7g, Saturated Fat 1g, Cholesterol 34g, Sodium 252mg, Total Carbohydrate 40.8g, Total Sugars 2g, Protein 8.3g

Keto Pumpkin Bread

Servings: 1 Loaf

Cooking Time: 1 Hour And 30 Minutes

Ingredients:
1 ½ cup almond flour
½ cup coconut flour
2/3 cup no-calorie sweetener of your choice
½ cup butter softened
One teaspoon cinnamon
½ teaspoon nutmeg
½ teaspoon salt
¼ teaspoon ginger, grated
1/8 teaspoon ground cloves
Four eggs
¾ cup pumpkin puree
Four teaspoons baking powder
One teaspoon vanilla extract

Directions:
Add the wet ingredients followed by dry ingredients into the bread pan.
Use the "Quick" or "Cake" mode of the bread machine.
Wait until the cycles are done.
Remove the pan from the machine, but take out the bread from the pan for 10 mins.
Let the bread cool down first before slicing it completely.

Nutrition Info: Calories: 242, Carbohydrates: 11g, Fat: 20g, Protein: 7g

White Chocolate Bread

Servings: 1 Loaf

Cooking Time: 2 Hours And 55 Minutes

Ingredients:
¼ cup warm water
1 cup warm milk
1 egg
¼ cup butter, softened
3 cups bread flour
2 tablespoons brown sugar
2 tablespoons white sugar
1 teaspoon salt
1 teaspoon ground cinnamon
1 (.25 ounce) package active dry yeast
1 cup white chocolate chips

Directions:
Place all ingredients (except the white chocolate chips) in the pan of the bread machine in the order recommended by the manufacturer. Select cycle; press Start.
If your machine has a Fruit setting, add the white chocolate chips at the signal, otherwise you can do it about 5 minutes before the kneading cycle has finished.

Nutrition Info: Calories 277, Protein 6.6g, Carbohydrates 39g, Fat: 10.5g

European Black Bread

Servings: 1 Loaf

Cooking Time: 1 Hour And 5 Minutes

Ingredients:
¾ teaspoon cider vinegar
1 cup of water
½ cup rye flour
1 ½ cups flour
One tablespoon margarine
¼ cup of oat bran
One teaspoon salt
1 ½ tablespoons sugar
One teaspoon dried onion flakes
One teaspoon caraway seed
One teaspoon yeast
Two tablespoons unsweetened cocoa

Directions:
Put everything in your bread machine.
Now select the basic setting.
Hit the start button.
Transfer bread to a rack for cooling once done.

Nutrition Info: Calories 114, Carbohydrates: 22g, Total Fat 1.7g, Cholesterol 0mg, Protein 3g, Sugar 2g, Sodium 247mg

Cinnamon Butter Cookies

Servings: 12 Pcs

Cooking Time: 12 Minutes

Ingredients:
2 cups Almond Flour
¼ tsp Salt
½ tsp Cinnamon Powder
One stick butter softened
1 tsp Vanilla Extract
½ cup Swerve Granular Sweetener
1 Whole Egg

Directions:
Preheat oven to 350F.
Put Whisk together the almond flour, salt, cinnamon, and sweetener in a bowl.
Cut in the butter until the mixture resembles a coarse meal.
Mix in the egg and vanilla extract.
Scoop the dough into a baking sheet lined with parchment. Press slightly to flatten.
Bake for 12 minutes.

Nutrition Info: Kcal per serve: 171, Fat: 16g, Protein: 4 g, Carbs: 3g

Portugese Sweet Bread

Servings: 1 Loaf

Cooking Time: 3 Hours

Ingredients:
1 cup milk
egg
tablespoons margarine
⅓ cup white sugar
¾ teaspoon salt
cups bread flour
2 ½ teaspoons active dry yeast

Directions:
Add ingredients in order suggested by your manufacturer.
Select "sweet bread" setting.

Nutrition Info: Calories 56, Protein 1.5g, Carbohydrates 6.9g,
Fat: 2.6g

British Hot Cross Buns

Servings: 12

Cooking Time: 2 Hours 30 Minutes

Ingredients:
3/4 cup warm milk
3 tablespoons butter, unsalted
1/4 cup white sugar
1/2 teaspoon salt
1 egg
1 egg white
3 cups all-purpose flour
1 tablespoon active dry yeast
3/4 cup dried raisins
1 teaspoon ground cinnamon
For Brushing:
egg yolk
tablespoons water
For the Crosses:
2 tablespoons flour
Cold water
1/2 tablespoon sugar

Directions:

Put milk, butter, 1/4 cup sugar, salt, egg, egg white, flour, and yeast in bread maker and start the Dough cycle.

Add raisins and cinnamon 5 minutes before kneading cycle ends.

Allow to rest in machine until doubled, about 30 minutes.

Punch down on a floured surface, cover, and let rest 10 minutes.

Shape into 12 balls and place in a greased 9-by-12-inch pan.

Cover and let rise in a warm place until doubled, about 35-40 minutes.

Mix egg yolk and 2 tablespoons water and baste each bun.

Mix the cross ingredients to form pastry.

Roll out pastry and cut into thin strips. Place across the buns to form crosses.

Bake at 375°F for 20 minutes.

Remove from pan immediately and cool on a rack. Serve warm.

Nutrition Info: Calories: 200, Sodium: 135mg, Dietary Fiber: 1.5g, Fat: 4g, Carbs: 36.5g, Protein: 5.2g

Amish Wheat Bread

Servings: 12

Cooking Time: 2 Hours 50 Minutes

Ingredients:
1 1/8 cups warm water
package active dry yeast
3/4 cups wheat flour
1/2 teaspoon salt
1/3 cup sugar
1/4 cup canola oil
1 large egg

Directions:
Add warm water, sugar and yeast to bread maker pan; let sit for 8 minutes or until it foams.
Add remaining ingredients to the pan.
Select Basic bread cycle, light crust color, and press Start.
Transfer to a cooling rack for 20 minutes before slicing.

Nutrition Info: Calories: 173, Sodium: 104mg, Dietary Fiber: 0.9g, Fat: 5.3g, Carbs: 27.7g, Protein: 3.7g

Swedish Cardamom Bread

Servings: 1 Loaf

Cooking Time: 15 Minutes

Ingredients:
¼ cup of sugar
¾ cup of warm milk
¾ teaspoon cardamom
½ teaspoon salt
¼ cup of softened butter
One egg
Two ¼ teaspoons bread machine yeast
3 cups all-purpose flour
Five tablespoons milk for brushing
Two tablespoons sugar for sprinkling

Directions:
Put everything (except milk for brushing and sugar for sprinkling) in the pan of your bread machine.
Select the dough cycle. Hit the start button. You should have an elastic and smooth dough once the process is complete. It should be double in size.
Transfer to a lightly floured surface.
Now divide into three balls. Set aside for 10 minutes.
Roll all the balls into long ropes of around 14 inches.
Braid the shapes. Pinch ends under securely and keeps on a cookie sheet. You can also divide your dough into two balls. Smooth them and keep on your bread pan.
Brush milk over the braid. Sprinkle sugar lightly.
Now bake in your oven for 25 minutes at 375 degrees F (190 degrees C).
Take a foil and cover for the final 10 minutes. It's prevents over-browning.
Transfer to your cooling rack.

Nutrition Info: Calories 135, Carbohydrates: 22g, Total Fat 7g, Cholesterol 20mg, Protein 3g, Fiber 1g, Sugar 3g, Sodium 100mg

Vanilla Milk Bread

Servings: 1 Loaf

Cooking Time: 3 Hours And 30 Minutes

Ingredients:
4½ cups (580 g) wheat bread machine flour
1¾ cups (370 ml / 12½ oz.) lukewarm whole milk
tbsp. white sugar
One packet vanilla sugar
tbsp. extra-virgin olive oil
2 tsp. bread machine yeast
2 tsp. sea salt

Directions:
Place all the dry and liquid ingredients in the pan and follow the instructions for your bread machine.
Pay particular attention to measuring the ingredients. Use a cup, measuring spoon, and kitchen scales to do so.
Set, the baking program to BASIC, also set the crust type to MEDIUM.
If the dough is too wet, adjust the recipe's flour and liquid quantity.
When the program has ended, take the pan out of the bread machine and cool for five minutes.
Shake the loaf out of the pan. If necessary, use a spatula.
Wrap the bread with a kitchen towel and set it aside for an hour. Otherwise, you'll calm on a wire rack.

Nutrition Info: Calories 328, Total Fat 5.7g, Saturated Fat 1.4g, Cholesterol 4g, Sodium 610mg, Carbohydrate 59.1g, Dietary Fiber 2.1g, Total Sugars 4.6g, Protein 9.4g

German Pumpernickel Bread

Servings: 1 Loaf

Cooking Time: 1 Hour And 10 Minutes

Ingredients:
1 1/2 tablespoon vegetable oil
1 1/8 cups warm water
Three tablespoons cocoa
1/3 cup molasses
1 ½ teaspoons salt
One tablespoon caraway seeds
1 cup rye flour
1 ½ cups of bread flour
1 ½ tablespoon wheat gluten
cup whole wheat flour
½ teaspoons bread machine yeast

Directions:
Put everything in your bread machine.
Select the primary cycle.
Hit the start button.
Transfer bread to a rack for cooling once done.

Nutrition Info: Calories 119, Carbohydrates: 22.4g, Total Fat 2.3 g, Cholesterol 0mg, Protein 3g, Sodium 295 mg

OTHER BREAD MACHINE RECIPES

Cocoa Banana Bread

Servings: 1 Loaf

Cooking Time: 10 Minutes

Ingredients:
12 slice bread (1½ pounds)
3 bananas, mashed
2 eggs, at room temperature
¾ cup packed light brown sugar
½ cup unsalted butter, melted
½ cup sour cream, at room temperature
¼ cup sugar
1½ teaspoons pure vanilla extract
cup all-purpose flour
½ cup quick oats
tablespoons unsweetened cocoa powder
1 teaspoon baking soda

Directions:
Preparing the Ingredients.
Choose the size of loaf of your preference and then measure the ingredients.
Add all of the ingredients mentioned previously in the list.
Close the lid after placing the pan in the bread machine.
Select the Bake cycle
Turn on the bread machine. Select the Quick/Rapid setting, select the loaf size, and the crust color. Press start.
When the cycle is finished, carefully remove the pan from the bread maker and let it rest.
Remove the bread from the pan, put in a wire rack to Cool about 5 minutes. Slice

Nutrition Info: 152 Calories, 3g Fat, 27g Carbs, 7g Protein

Swedish Coffee Bread

Servings: 14 Slices

Cooking Time: 10 Minutes

Ingredients:
1 cup milk
½ tsp salt
egg yolk
Tbsp softened butter
cups all-purpose flour
⅓ cup sugar
1 envelope active dry yeast
3 tsp ground cardamom
2 egg whites, slightly beaten

Directions:
Preparing the Ingredients
Add each ingredient to the bread machine in the order and at the temperature recommended by your bread machine manufacturer.
Select the Bake cycle
Select the dough cycle and press start. Grease your baking sheet.
When the dough cycle has finished, divide the dough into three equal parts. Roll each part into a rope 12-14" long. Lay 3 ropes side by side, and then braid them together.
Tuck the ends underneath and put onto the sheet. Next, cover the bread, using kitchen towel, and let it rise until it has doubled in size. Brush your bread with beaten egg white and sprinkle with pearl sugar. Bake until golden brown at 375°F in a preheated oven for 20-25 minutes. When baked, remove the bread and put it on a cooling rack.

Nutrition Info: 152 Calories, 3.4g Fat, 32g Carbs, 5g Protein

Quinoa Oatmeal Bread

Servings: 6 to 8 servings

Cooking Time: 3 hrs 30 mins

Ingredients:
1/3 cup quinoa (uncooked; or 1/2 cup quinoa flakes)
2/3 cup water (for cooking quinoa)
1 cup buttermilk
1 1/2 cups bread flour
1/2 cup whole wheat flour
1/2 cup quick-cooking oats
4 tablespoons (1/2 stick) unsalted butter (melted and cooled)
1 tablespoon sugar
1 tablespoon honey
1 1/2 teaspoons yeast
1 teaspoon salt

Directions:
To a saucepan, add the quinoa and cover it with the water. (If using quinoa flakes instead of raw quinoa, skip this step). Bring to a boil and cook for 5 minutes, covered. Turn off the heat and let quinoa sit, covered, for 10 minutes.
Check your bread machine directions for the correct order to add the ingredients. Add the buttermilk, bread flour, whole wheat flour, oats, butter, sugar, honey, yeast, and salt (in an order specified by the manual) to the bread machine, including the cooked quinoa (or quinoa flakes).
Program the machine for a whole grain loaf and let the bread machine cycle and bake.
Let the bread cool for at least 15 minutes before slicing. Enjoy!

Nutrition Info: 295 Calories, 14g Fat, 37g Carbs, 6g Protein

Cheesebuttermilk Bread

Servings: 10

Cooking Time: 2 Hours

Ingredients:
Buttermilk – 1 1/8 cups
Active dry yeast – 1 ½ tsps.
Cheddar cheese – ¾ cup., shredded
Sugar – 1 ½ tsps.
Bread flour – 3 cups.
Buttermilk – 1 1/8 cups.
Salt – 1 1/2 tsps.

Directions:
Add all ingredients to the bread machine pan according to the bread machine manufacturer instructions. Select basic bread setting then select light/medium crust and start. Once loaf is done, remove the loaf pan from the machine. Allow it to cool for 10 minutes. Slice and serve.

Nutrition Info: 275 Calories, 12g Fat, 33g Carbs, 7g Protein

Peanut Butter Bread

Servings: 10

Cooking Time: 40 mins

Ingredients:
1 cup plus 1 tablespoon water
1/2 cup peanut butter
3 cups bread flour
3 tablespoons brown sugar
1 teaspoon salt
2 teaspoons yeast (bread machine)

Directions:
Measuring carefully, place the water, peanut butter, bread flour, brown sugar, salt, and bread machine yeast in the bread machine in the order recommended by the manufacturer.
place the water, peanut butter, bread flour, brown sugar, salt, and bread machine yeast in the bread machine
Select "Sweet" or "Basic/White" cycle. Use "Medium" or "Light Crust Color" and turn the machine on. When the bread is finished it should be a dark gold color and should sound hollow when you tap it with your fingers. You can also test the temperature of the bread; it should be about 210 F.
peanut butter bread in a bread machine
Carefully remove the bread from the bread machine pan and cool on a wire rack.
Peanut Butter Bread on a wire cooling rack

Nutrition Info: 136 Calories, 8g Fat, 14g Carbs, 4g Protein

Jalapeno Cheddar Bread

Servings: 1 Loaf

Ingredients:
16 slice bread (2 pounds)
1⅓ cups lukewarm buttermilk
⅓ cup unsalted butter, melted
2 eggs, at room temperature
⅔ teaspoon table salt
jalapeno pepper, chopped
⅔ cup Cheddar cheese, shredded
⅓ cup sugar
cups all-purpose flour
1⅓ cups cornmeal
1½ tablespoons baking powder
12 slice bread (1½ pounds)
1 cup lukewarm buttermilk
¼ cup unsalted butter, melted
2 eggs, at room temperature
½ teaspoon table salt
1 jalapeno pepper, chopped
½ cup Cheddar cheese, shredded
¼ cup sugar
1⅓ cups all-purpose flour
1 cup cornmeal
1 tablespoon baking powder

Directions:

Choose the size of loaf you would like to make and measure your ingredients.

Add the ingredients to the bread pan in the order listed above.

Place the pan in the bread machine and close the lid.

Turn on the bread maker. Select the Rapid/Quick setting, then the loaf size, and finally the crust color. Start the cycle.

When the cycle is finished and the bread is baked, carefully remove the pan from the machine. Use a potholder as the handle will be very hot. Let rest for a few minutes.

Remove the bread from the pan and allow to cool on a wire rack for at least 10 minutes before slicing.

Nutrition Info: (Per Serving): Calories 173, fat 6.2g, carbs 24.3g, sodium 187mg, protein 4.8g

Slider Buns

Servings: 18

Cooking Time: 17 mins

Ingredients:
1 (1/4-ounce) package (2 1/4 teaspoons) active dry yeast
1/2 cup water, warm, about 110 F
2/3 cup milk, room temperature
1 large egg
3 tablespoons butter, melted and cooled slightly
2 1/2 tablespoons sugar
1 1/4 teaspoons salt
3 cups all-purpose flour (dip and sweep method)
Butter or oil, for greasing the bowl
Optional Toppings:
1 large egg white
1 tablespoon water
1/4 cup sesame seeds or poppy seeds
Melted butter

Directions:

Combine the yeast and warm water in a bowl. Let the mixture stand for about 10 minutes, until foamy.

In a small bowl, whisk together the milk, melted butter, and egg.
Milk, melted butter, and egg in a bowl

Place the milk mixture along with the flour, sugar, salt, and yeast mixture in the bread machine in the order suggested by the manufacturer.
Milk mixture, flour, salt, and yeast in a bread machine

Set to the dough cycle.
Set bread machine to the dough cycle

Remove the finished dough to a lightly floured surface. Flatten into a rectangle, cut into pieces, and shape the dough into balls. Place on a parchment-lined baking sheet, cover with a kitchen towel, and let rise for 30 minutes.
Cover buns

Brush with the egg wash and seeds, if using, and bake in a 375 F oven for 15 to 18 minutes.
Bake buns

If desired, brush with melted butter if the egg wash and seeds weren't used. Let the buns cool on a rack.
Let buns cool

Split the buns in half, add sandwich fillings, and enjoy.

Nutrition Info: 134 Calories, 5g Fat, 19g Carbs, 4g Protein

Onion Bread

Servings: 12

Cooking Time: 2 hrs

Ingredients:
1-1/2 cups water
2 tablespoons plus
2 teaspoons butter
1-1/2 teaspoons salt
1 tablespoon plus 1-1/2 teaspoons sugar
4 cups bread flour
2 tablespoons plus 2 teaspoons nonfat dry milk
2 teaspoons active dry yeast
3-4 tablespoons dry onion soup mix

Directions:
Place ingredients in bread pan in order listed or according to manufacturer's directions.
The onion soup mix is added at the fruit and nut signal. Depending on your machine this could be anywhere from 30 to 40 minutes into the cycle.

Nutrition Info: 130 Calories, 3g Fat, 16g Carbs, 8g Protein

Hamburger Buns

Servings: 8

Cooking Time: 18 mins

Ingredients:
1 1/3 cups water
2 tablespoons nonfat milk powder
4 cups all-purpose flour, plus more for kneading
2 tablespoons shortening
2 1/2 to 3 tablespoons sugar
2 teaspoons salt
1 packet active dry yeast (about 2 1/2 teaspoons)
Cornmeal, for sprinkling baking sheet
1 egg white, whisked with 1 tablespoon of water
2 tablespoons sesame seeds or poppy seeds

Directions:

Add the water and nonfat milk powder to the bread machine followed by the flour. Add the shortening followed by the sugar, salt, and yeast. Set to the "dough" cycle.

When the dough cycle finishes, turn the dough out onto a floured board and punch it down. Knead 4 or 5 times; add a little more flour as you knead if necessary to keep the dough from sticking to your hands or the board.

Cover the dough with a clean dishcloth and let it rest for about 30 minutes in a draft-free place.

Lightly grease a large baking sheet; sprinkle with cornmeal. Alternatively, line the baking sheet with parchment paper and sprinkle with cornmeal.

Pat the dough into a circle and cut into 8 even wedges. Form each wedge into a ball, then flatten each one into a smooth and fairly even circle, slightly bigger than a burger.

Arrange the dough pieces on the baking sheet about 2 inches apart and let rest for about 20 minutes.

Preheat the oven to 375 F.

Brush the buns lightly with the egg wash (egg and water mixture). If desired, sprinkle with sesame seeds or poppy seeds.

Bake for about 18 minutes or until the buns are nicely browned.

Let cool before serving.

Nutrition Info: 293 Calories, 5g Fat, 54g Carbs, 8g Protein

Raisin Bread

Servings: 15

Cooking Time: 3 Hours And 25 Minutes

Ingredients:
Coconut flour – ½ cup
Almond flour – ½ cup
Psyllium husk powder - 6 tbsp.
Chopped raisins – ¼ cup
Swerve – 2 tbsp.
Baking powder – 1 tbsp.
Ground cinnamon – ½ tsp.
Salt, to taste – ¼ tsp.
Egg whites - 2 cups
Butter – 3 tbsp., melted
Apple cider vinegar – 2 tbsp.

Directions:
Add everything in the bread machine in the order recommended by the machine manufacturer.
Select Basic bread setting and choose crust. Press Start.
Remove the bread when done.
Cool, slice, and serve.

Nutrition Info: (Per Serving): Calories: 120, Total Fat: 4g, Saturated Fat: 2.3g, Carbohydrates: 9g, Cholesterol: 6mg, Fiber: 11.1g, Calcium: 48mg, Sodium: 89mg, Protein: 5.4g

Loaf of Gluten-Free Sandwiches

Servings: 9

Cooking Time: 2 Hours

Ingredients:
cup warm water
tablespoons butter, unsalted
1 egg, room temperature
teaspoon apple cider vinegar
3/4 cups gluten-free almond-blend flour
1 1/2 teaspoons xanthan gum
1/4 cup sugar
teaspoon salt
teaspoons active dry yeast

Directions:
Add wet ingredients to the bread maker pan.
Mix dry ingredients except for yeast, and put in pan.
Make a well in the center of the dry ingredients and add the yeast.
Select Dough cycle and press Start.
Spray an 8-inch round cake pan with non-stick cooking spray.
When Dough cycle is complete, roll dough out into 9 balls, place in cake pan, and baste each with warm water.
Cover with a towel and let rise in a warm place for 1 hour.
Preheat oven to 400°F.
Bake for 26 to 28 minutes; until golden brown.
Brush with butter and serve.

Nutrition Info: Calories: 568, Sodium: 380mg, Dietary Fiber: 5.5g, Fat: 10.5g, Carbs: 116.3g, Protein: 8.6g.

Banana and Lemon Bread

Servings: 1 Loaf (16 Slices)

Cooking Time: 1 Hour And 30 Minutes

Ingredients:
2 cups all-purpose flour
1 cup bananas, very ripe and mashed
1 cup walnuts, chopped
1 cup of sugar
One tablespoon baking powder
One teaspoon lemon peel, grated
½ teaspoon salt
Two eggs
½ cup of vegetable oil
Two tablespoons lemon juice

Directions:
Put all ingredients into a pan in this order: bananas, wet ingredients, and then dry ingredients.
Press the "Quick" or "Cake" setting of your bread machine.
Allow the cycles to be completed.
Take out the pan from the machine. The cooldown for 10 minutes before slicing the bread enjoy.

Nutrition Info: Calories: 120, Carbohydrates: 15g, Fat: 6g, Protein: 2g

Cheese and Herb Bread

Servings: 1 Loaf

Ingredients:
16 slice bread (2 pounds)
1⅓ cups lukewarm water
2 tablespoons olive oil
1 teaspoon table salt
tablespoon sugar
cloves garlic, crushed
tablespoons mixed fresh herbs (basil, chives, oregano, rosemary, etc.)
¼ cup Parmesan cheese, grated
cups white bread flour
2¼ teaspoons bread machine yeast
12 slice bread (1½ pounds)
cup lukewarm water
1½ tablespoons olive oil
¾ teaspoon table salt
¾ tablespoon sugar
cloves garlic, crushed
tablespoons mixed fresh herbs (basil, chives, oregano, rosemary, etc.)
tablespoons Parmesan cheese, grated
3 cups white bread flour
1⅔ teaspoons bread machine yeast

Directions:

Choose the size of loaf you would like to make and measure your ingredients.

Add the ingredients to the bread pan in the order listed above.

Place the pan in the bread machine and close the lid.

Turn on the bread maker. Select the White/Basic setting, then the loaf size, and finally the crust color. Start the cycle.

When the cycle is finished and the bread is baked, carefully remove the pan from the machine. Use a potholder as the handle will be very hot. Let rest for a few minutes.

Remove the bread from the pan and allow to cool on a wire rack for at least 10 minutes before slicing.

Nutrition Info: (Per Serving): Calories 147, fat 3.2g, carbs 25.3g, sodium 37mg, protein 5.1g

Sun Vegetable Bread

Servings: 8 Pcs

Cooking Time: 1 Hour And 30 Minutes

Ingredients:
2 cups (250 g) wheat flour
2 cups (250 g) whole-wheat flour
Two teaspoons yeast
1½ teaspoons salt
One tablespoon sugar
One tablespoon paprika dried slices
Two tablespoons dried beets
One tablespoon dried garlic
1½ cups water
One tablespoon vegetable oil

Directions:
The set baking program, which should be 4 hours, crust colour, is medium.
Be sure to look at the kneading phase of the dough to get a smooth and soft bun.

Nutrition Info: Calories 253, Total Fat 2.6g, Saturated Fat 0.5g, Cholesterol 0g, Sodium 444mg, Total Sugars 0.6g, Protein 7.2g

Milk And Honey Bread

Servings: 12

Cooking Time: 2 Hours And 10 Minutes

Ingredients:
Warm milk – 1 ½ cups
Unsalted butter – ¼ cup
Eggs – 2, beaten
Apple cider vinegar – 1 tsp.
Honey – ½ cup
All-purpose gluten-free flour – 3 cups
Salt – 1 tsp.
Xanthan gum – 1 ½ tsp
Instant yeast – 1 ¾ tsp.

Directions:
Add everything according to bread machine recommendations.
Select Gluten-Free setting.
Remove the bread when done.
Cool, slice, and serve.

Nutrition Info: (Per Serving): Calories: 212, Total Fat: 6g,
Saturated Fat: 3g, Carbohydrates: 35g, Cholesterol: 40mg, Fiber: 3g,
Calcium: 61mg, Sodium: 263mg, Protein: 5g

Spiced Herb Bread

Servings: 1 Loaf

Cooking Time: 10 Minutes

Ingredients:
8 slice bread (1 pound)
1⅓ cups No-Yeast Sourdough Starter, fed, active, and at room temperature
4 teaspoons water, at 80°F to 90°F
4 teaspoons melted butter, cooled
1⅓ teaspoons sugar
1 teaspoon salt
1 teaspoon chopped fresh basil
1 teaspoon chopped fresh oregano
½ teaspoon chopped fresh thyme
1⅔ cups white bread flour
1 teaspoon bread machine or instant yeast

Directions:
Preparing the Ingredients.
Choose the size of loaf of your preference and then measure the ingredients.
Add all of the ingredients mentioned previously in the list, close the lid after placing the pan in the bread machine
Select the Bake cycle
Turn on the bread machine. Select the Wheat/Whole-Grain bread setting, select the loaf size, and the crust color. Press start. When the cycle is finished, carefully remove the pan from the bread maker and let it rest.
Remove the bread from the pan, put in a wire rack to cool for at least 5 minutes, and slice

Nutrition Info: Calories: 146, Carbohydrates: 33g, Fat: 5g, Protein: 4g

Whole Wheat Bread Gluten Free

Servings: 12

Cooking Time: 3 Hours

Ingredients:
2 large eggs, lightly beaten
1 3/4 cups warm water
3 tablespoons canola oil
1 cup brown rice flour
3/4 cup oat flour
1/4 cup tapioca starch
1 1/4 cups potato starch
1/2 teaspoons salt
tablespoons brown sugar
2 tablespoons gluten-free flaxseed meal
1/2 cup nonfat dry milk powder
1/2 teaspoons xanthan gum
tablespoons psyllium, whole husks
2 1/2 teaspoons gluten-free yeast for bread machines

Directions:
Add the eggs, water and canola oil to the bread maker pan and stir until combined.
Whisk all of the dry ingredients except the yeast together in a large mixing bowl.
Add the dry ingredients on top of the wet ingredients.
Make a well in the center of the dry ingredients and add the yeast.
Set Gluten-Free cycle, medium crust color, and press Start.
When the bread is done, lay the pan on its side to cool before slicing to serve.

Nutrition Info: Calories: 201, Sodium: 390mg, Dietary Fiber: 10.6g, Fat: 5.7g, Carbs: 35.5g, Protein: 5.1g

Corn Bread

Servings: 1 Loaf

Cooking Time: 10 Minutes

Ingredients:
12 to 16 slices bread (1½ to 2 pounds)
cup buttermilk, at 80°F to 90°F
¼ cup melted butter, cooled
eggs, at room temperature
1⅓ cups all-purpose flour
1 cup cornmeal
¼ cup sugar
2¼ cups whole-wheat bread flour
1½ teaspoons bread machine yeast

Directions:
Preparing the Ingredients.
Place the buttermilk, butter, and eggs in your in your bread machine as recommended by the manufacturer.
Select the Bake cycle
Program the machine for Quick/Rapid bread and press Start. While the wet ingredients are mixing, stir together the flour, cornmeal, sugar, baking powder, and salt in a small bowl.
After the first fast mixing is done and the machine signals, add the dry ingredients.
When the loaf is done, remove the bucket from the machine. Let the loaf cool for 5 minutes.
Gently shake the bucket to remove the loaf, and turn it out onto a rack to cool.

Nutrition Info: Calories: 156, Carbohydrates: 39g, Fat: 5.3g, Protein: 4g

Low-sodium Bread

Servings: 12

Cooking Time: 3 Hours And 25 Minutes

Ingredients:
Warm water – 1 cup
Unsalted butter – 2 tbsp.
Dry milk – 1 tbsp.
All-purpose flour – 3 cups
Bread machine yeast – 1 tsp.

Directions:
Add everything according to bread machine recommendations.
Select Basic cycle and crust color.
Remove the bread when done.
Cool, slice, and serve.

Nutrition Info: (Per Serving): Calories: 143.9, Total Fat: 2.7g, Saturated Fat: 1.4g, Carbohydrates: 25.1g, Cholesterol: 5.8mg, Fiber: 0.8g, Calcium: 28mg, Sodium: 3.5mg, Protein: 4.3g

No-yeast Sourdough Starter

Servings: 4 Cups

Cooking Time: 10 Minutes Plus Fermenting Time

Ingredients:
2 cups all-purpose flour
2 cups chlorine-free bottled water, at room temperature

Directions:
Preparing the Ingredients.
Stir together the flour and water in a large glass bowl with a wooden spoon. Loosely cover the bowl with plastic wrap and place it in a warm area for 3 to 4 days, stirring at least twice a day, or until bubbly.
Select the Bake cycle
Store the starter in the refrigerator in a covered glass jar, and stir it before using.
Replenish your starter by adding back the same amount you removed, in equal parts flour and water.

Nutrition Info: Calories: 121 Cal, Fat: 3.2g, Carb: 11.1g, Protein: 4.3g

Gluten Free Bread for Sandwiches

Servings: 12

Cooking Time: 1 Hour

Ingredients:
1 1/2 cups sorghum flour
cup tapioca starch or potato starch (not potato flour!)
1/2 cup gluten-free millet flour or gluten-free oat flour
teaspoons xanthan gum
1/4 teaspoons fine sea salt
1/2 teaspoons gluten-free yeast for bread machines
1 1/4 cups warm water
3 tablespoons extra virgin olive oil
tablespoon honey or raw agave nectar
1/2 teaspoon mild rice vinegar or lemon juice
organic free-range eggs, beaten

Directions:
Whisk together the dry ingredients except the yeast and set aside.
Add the liquid ingredients to the bread maker pan first, then gently
pour the mixed dry ingredients on top of the liquid.
Make a well in the center of the dry ingredients and add the yeast.
Set for Rapid 1 hour 20 minutes, medium crust color, and press Start.
Transfer to a cooling rack for 15 minutes before slicing to serve.

Nutrition Info: Calories: 137, Sodium: 85mg, Dietary Fiber: 2.7g,
Fat: 4.6g, Carbs: 22.1g, Protein: 2.4g.

Chocolate Zucchini Bread

Servings: 1 Loaf

Cooking Time: 10 Minutes

Ingredients:
225 grams grated zucchini
125 grams All-Purpose Flour Blend
50 grams all-natural unsweetened cocoa powder (not Dutch-process)
1 teaspoon xanthan gum
¾ teaspoon baking soda
¼ teaspoon baking powder
¼ teaspoon salt
½ teaspoon ground espresso
135 grams chocolate chips or nondairy alternative
100 grams cane sugar or granulated sugar
2 large eggs
¼ cup avocado oil or canola oil
60 grams vanilla Greek yogurt or nondairy alternative
1 teaspoon vanilla extract

Directions:
Preparing the Ingredients.
Measure and add the ingredients to the pan in the order mentioned above. Place the pan in the bread machine and close the lid.
Select the Bake cycle
Turn on the bread maker. Select the White / Basic setting, then select the dough size, select light or medium crust. Press start to start the cycle.
When this is done, and the bread is baked, remove the pan from the machine. Let stand a few minutes.
Remove the bread from the skillet and leave it on a wire rack to cool for at least 15 minutes. Store leftovers in an airtight container at room temperature for up to 5 days, or freeze to enjoy a slice whenever you desire. Let each slice thaw naturally

Nutrition Info: Calories: 132 Cal, Fat: 5.2g, Carb: 14.1g, Protein: 4.3g

Bread with Spinach and Feta

Servings: 14 Slices

Cooking Time: 10 Minutes

Ingredients:
1 cup water
tsp butter
cups flour
tsp sugar
tsp instant minced onion
1 tsp salt
1¼ tsp instant yeast
1 cup crumbled feta
1 cup chopped fresh spinach leaves

Directions:
Preparing the Ingredients
Add each ingredient except the cheese and spinach to the bread machine in the order and at the temperature recommended by your bread machine manufacturer.
Select the Bake cycle
Close the lid, select the basic bread, medium crust setting on your bread machine, and press start.
When only 10 minutes are left in the last kneading cycle add the spinach and cheese.
When the bread machine has finished baking, remove the bread and put it on a cooling rack.

Bread with Pumpkin and Raisins

Servings: 1 Loaf

Cooking Time: 10 Minutes

Ingredients:
16 slice bread (2 pounds)
2 cups cooked mashed butternut squash, at room temperature
1 cup (2 sticks) butter, at room temperature
3 eggs, at room temperature
teaspoon pure vanilla extract
cups sugar
½ cup light brown sugar
cups all-purpose flour
1 teaspoon baking soda
1 teaspoon ground cinnamon
½ teaspoon ground cloves
½ teaspoon ground nutmeg
½ teaspoon salt
½ teaspoon baking powder
½ cup golden raisins

Directions:
Preparing the Ingredients.
Place the butternut squash, butter, eggs, vanilla, sugar, and brown sugar
in your bread machine.
Select the Bake cycle
Program the machine for Quick/Rapid bread and press Start.
While the wet ingredients are mixing, stir together the flour, baking
soda, cinnamon, cloves, nutmeg, salt, and baking powder in a small
bowl.
After the first fast mixing is done and the machine signals, add the dry
ingredients and raisins.
When the cycle is finished, carefully remove the pan from the bread
maker and let it rest. 8.   Remove the bread from the pan, put in a wire
rack to Cool about 5 minutes. Slice

No-salt White Bread

Servings: 12

Cooking Time: 3 Hours And 25 Minutes

Ingredients:
Warm water - 1 cup
Olive oil – 1 tbsp.
Sugar – 1 ¼ tsp.
Yeast – 1 ¼ tsp.
Flour – 3 ¼ cup
Egg white - 1

Directions:
Dissolve the sugar in the water.
Add yeast to the sugar water.
Put flour, yeast mixture, and oil into the bread-maker.
Select Basic bread setting.
Add the egg white after 5 minutes.
Remove the bread when it is done.
Cool, slice, and serve.

Nutrition Info: (Per Serving): Calories: 275.3, Total Fat: 3 g,
Saturated Fat: 0.4 g, Carbohydrates: 52.9 g, Cholesterol: 0 mg,
Fiber: 2 g, Calcium: 22 mg, Sodium: 12.2 mg Protein: 7.9 g

Rosemary Bread

Servings: 8 Pcs

Cooking Time: 1 Hour

Ingredients:
300ml (1 ¼ cups) warm water
60ml (¼ cup) olive oil
Two egg whites
One tablespoon apple cider vinegar
½ teaspoon baking powder
Two teaspoons dry active yeast
Two tablespoons granulated sugar
½ teaspoon Italian seasoning
¼ teaspoon ground black pepper
1¼ teaspoon dried rosemary
200g (2 cups) gluten-free almond flour / or any other gluten-free flour, levelled
100g (1 cup) Tapioca/potato starch, levelled
Two teaspoons Xanthan Gum
One teaspoon salt

Directions:
According to your bread machine manufacturer, place all the ingredients into the bread machine's greased pan.
Select basic cycle / standard cycle/bake / quick bread / white bread setting then choose crust color either medium or Light and press start to bake bread. In the last kneading cycle, check the dough it should be wet but thick, not like traditional bread dough. If the dough is too wet, put more flour, one tablespoon at a time, or until dough slightly firm. When the cycle is finished, and the baker machine turns off, remove baked bread from pan and cool on wire rack.

Nutrition Info: Calories: 150, Calories, Total fat: 3g, Cholesterol: 5mg, Sodium: 290mg, Carbohydrates: 24g, Fibre: 1g, Protein: 6g

Sweet Pineapple Bread

Servings: 1 Loaf

Cooking Time: 10 Minutes Plus Fermenting Time

Ingredients:
16 slice bread (2 pounds)
6 tablespoons unsalted butter, melted
2 eggs, at room temperature
½ cup coconut milk, at room temperature
½ cup pineapple juice, at room temperature
cup sugar
1½ teaspoons coconut extract
cups all-purpose flour
¾ cup shredded sweetened coconut
1 teaspoon baking powder
½ teaspoon table salt

Directions:
Preparing the Ingredients.
Place the ingredients, except the apple, in your bread machine as recommended by the manufacturer.
Select the Bake cycle
Program the machine for Quick/Rapid bread, select light or medium crust, and press Start.
Add the apple when the machine signals or 5 minutes before the last kneading cycle is complete.
When the cycle is finished, carefully remove the pan from the bread maker and let it rest.
Remove the bread from the pan, put in a wire rack to Cool about 5 minutes. Slice

Semolina Bread

Servings: 1 Loaf (16 Slices)

Cooking Time: 30 Minutes

Ingredients:
1 cup lukewarm water (80 degrees F)
One teaspoon salt
2½ tablespoons butter, melted
2½ teaspoons white sugar
2¼ cups all-purpose flour
1/3 cups semolina
1½ teaspoons active dry yeast

Directions:
Prepare all of the ingredients for your bread and measuring means (a cup, a spoon, kitchen scales).
Carefully measure the ingredients into the pan.
Put all the ingredients into a bread bucket in the right order. Follow your manual for the bread machine.
Close the cover.
Select your bread machine's program to ITALIAN BREAD / SANDWICH mode and choose the crust colour to MEDIUM.
Press START. Wait until the program completes.
When done, take the bucket out and let it cool for 5-10 minutes.
Shake the loaf from the pan and let cool for 30 minutes on a cooling rack.
Slice and serve.

Nutrition Info: Calories 243, Total Fat 8.1g, Saturated Fat 4.9g, Cholesterol 20g, Sodium 203mg, Total Carbohydrate 37g, Dietary Fiber 1.5g, Total Sugars 2.8g, Protein 5.3g

Vanilla Bread

Servings: 1 Loaf

Cooking Time: 10 Minutes Plus Fermenting Time

Ingredients:
12 slice bread (1½ pounds)
½ cup + 1 tablespoon lukewarm milk
3 tablespoons unsalted butter, melted
3 tablespoons sugar
1 egg, at room temperature
1½ teaspoons pure vanilla extract
⅓ teaspoon almond extract
2½ cups white bread flour
1½ teaspoons bread machine yeast

Directions:
Preparing the Ingredients.
Choose the size of loaf you would like to make and measure your ingredients.
Add the ingredients to the bread pan in the order listed above.
Place the pan in the bread machine and close the lid.
Select the Bake cycle
Turn on the bread maker. Select the White/Basic setting, then the loaf size, and finally the crust color. Start the cycle.
When the cycle is finished and the bread is baked, carefully remove the pan from the machine. Use a potholder as the handle will be very hot.
Let rest for a few minutes.
Remove the bread from the pan and allow to cool on a wire rack for at least 10 minutes before slicing.

Nutrition Info: Calories: 190, Carbohydrates: 6.3g, Protein: 7.1g, Fat: 18g

Potato Honey Bread

Servings: 1 Loaf

Cooking Time: 10 Minutes

Ingredients:
12 slice bread (1½ pounds)
¾ cup lukewarm water
½ cup finely mashed potatoes, at room temperature
egg, at room temperature
¼ cup unsalted butter, melted
tablespoons honey
1 teaspoon table salt
3 cups white bread flour
2 teaspoons bread machine yeast

Directions:
Preparing the Ingredients.
Choose the size of loaf of your preference and then measure the ingredients.
Add all of the ingredients mentioned previously in the list.
Close the lid after placing the pan in the bread machine.
Select the Bake cycle
Turn on the bread machine. Select the White/Basic setting, select the loaf size, and the crust color. Press start.
When the cycle is finished, carefully remove the pan from the bread maker and let it rest.
Remove the bread from the pan, put in a wire rack to Cool about 10 minutes. Slice

Nutrition Info: Calories: 174, Carbohydrates: 8g, Protein: 9g, Fat: 18g

Sausage Herb And Onion Bread

Servings: 14 Slices

Cooking Time: 3 H. 10 Min.
¾ tsp basil leaves
1½ Tbsp sugar
⅜ cup wheat bran
1 medium onion, minced
2¼ tsp yeast
¾ tsp rosemary leaves
½ Tbsp salt
1½ Tbsp parmesan, grated
3 cups bread flour
¾ tsp oregano leaves
¾ tsp thyme leaves
1⅛ cups water
¾ cup Italian sausage

Directions:
Remove casing from sausage. Crumble the meat into a medium nonstick skillet.
Cook on medium heat, stirring and breaking up sausage until it begins to render its juices.
Add onion and cook for 2-3 minuts until it softens and the sausage is no longer pink.
Remove from heat and let it cool.
Add each ingredient to the bread machine in the order and at the temperature recommended by your bread machine manufacturer.
Close the lid, select the basic bread, medium crust setting on your bread machine, and press start.
When the bread machine has finished baking, remove the bread and put it on a cooling rack.

Nutrition Info: Calories: 201, Carbohydrates: 9.2g, Protein: 7.3g, Fat: 18g

Anise Lemon Bread

Servings: 1 Loaf

Cooking Time: 10 Minutes

Ingredients:
12 slice bread (1½ pounds)
¾ cup water, at 80°F to 90°F
1 egg, at room temperature
¼ cup butter, melted and cooled
¼ cup honey
½ teaspoon salt
1 teaspoon anise seed
1 teaspoon lemon zest
3 cups white bread flour
2 teaspoons bread machine or instant yeast

Directions:
Preparing the Ingredients.
Choose the size of loaf of your preference and then measure the ingredients.
Add all of the ingredients mentioned previously in the list.
Close the lid after placing the pan in the bread machine.
Select the Bake cycle
Turn on the bread machine. Select the White/Basic setting, select the loaf size, and the crust color. Press start.
When the cycle is finished, carefully remove the pan from the bread maker and let it rest.
Remove the bread from the pan, put in a wire rack to Cool about 10 minutes. Slice

Nutrition Info: Calories: 184, Carbohydrates: 7g, Protein: 5g, Fat: 19g

Rice Flour Bread

Servings: 16 Slices

Cooking Time: 3 H. 15 Min.

Ingredients:
3 eggs
1½ cups water
3 Tbsp vegetable oil
1 tsp apple cider vinegar
2¼ tsp active dry yeast
3¼ cups white rice flour
2½ tsp xanthan gum
1½ tsp salt
½ cup dry milk powder
3 Tbsp white sugar

Directions:
In a medium-size bowl, mix the eggs, water, oil, and vinegar.
In a large bowl, add the yeast, salt, xanthan gum, dry milk powder, rice
flour, and sugar. Mix with a whisk until incorporated.
Add each ingredient to the bread machine in the order and at the
temperature recommended by your bread machine manufacturer.
Close the lid, select the whole wheat, medium crust setting on your
bread machine, and press start.
When the bread machine has finished baking, remove the bread and
put it on a cooling rack.

Nutrition Info: Calories: 154, Carbohydrates: 4.5g, Protein: 7.6g, Fat:
16g

Parmesan Cheese Bread

Servings: 1 Loaf

Cooking Time: 10 Minutes Plus Fermenting Time

Ingredients:
12 slice bread (1½ pounds)
1¼ cups lukewarm milk
tablespoon unsalted butter, melted
tablespoons sugar
1 teaspoon table salt
½ teaspoon freshly ground black pepper
Pinch cayenne pepper
1½ cups shredded aged sharp Cheddar cheese
½ cup shredded or grated Parmesan cheese
3 cups white bread flour
1¼ teaspoons bread machine yeast

Directions:
Preparing the Ingredients.
Choose the size of loaf of your preference and then measure the ingredients.
Add all of the ingredients mentioned previously in the list.
Close the lid after placing the pan in the bread machine.
Select the Bake cycle
Turn on the bread machine. Select the Quick/Rapid setting, select the loaf size, and the crust color. Press start.
When the cycle is finished, carefully remove the pan from the bread maker and let it rest.
Remove the bread from the pan, put in a wire rack to Cool about 5 minutes. Slice

Nutrition Info: Calories: 189, Carbohydrates: 7g, Protein: 9g, Fat: 19g

Blueberry Bread

Servings: 1 Loaf

Cooking Time: 10 Minutes

Ingredients:
12 to 16 slices (1½ to 2 pounds)
1 cup plain Greek yogurt, at room temperature
½ cup milk, at room temperature
3 tablespoons butter, at room temperature
2 eggs, at room temperature
½ cup sugar
¼ cup light brown sugar
teaspoon pure vanilla extract
½ teaspoon lemon zest
cups all-purpose flour
1 tablespoon baking powder
¾ teaspoon salt
¼ teaspoon ground nutmeg
1 cup blueberries

Directions:
Preparing the Ingredients.
Place the yogurt, milk, butter, eggs, sugar, brown sugar, vanilla, and zest in your bread machine.
Select the Bake cycle.
Program the machine for Quick/Rapid bread and press Start. While the wet ingredients are mixing, stir together the flour, baking powder, salt, and nutmeg in a medium bowl. After the first fast mixing is done and the machine signals, add the dry ingredients. When the second mixing cycle is complete, stir in the blueberries. When the loaf is done, remove the bucket from the machine. Let the loaf cool for 5 minutes. Gently shake the bucket to remove the loaf, and turn it out onto a rack to cool.

Nutrition Info: Calories: 212, Carbohydrates: 8.3g, Protein: 6.9g, Fat: 18g